Oracle E-Business Suite Upgrades & Implementations

StreetSmarts® What Scripts

Project Management, Technical and Functional Experts
Guiding You Down the Road to Success!

Version 6.1 Bill Dunham and Michael Barone

Published by Oracle Applications and Technology Consulting (OATC)

Jamison Park
3725 Grandbridge Drive
Apex, NC, USA 27539
(919) 326-3962

Current Edition : 12/28/2016

http://www.oatcinc.com/
http://oatcinc.blogspot.com/
Twitter : @OATCInc
LinkedIn: OATC, Inc.

Special Thanks to (alphabetically-ordered) Frank Bender, Tom Blanford, Sridhar Bommareddy, Mark Coleman, Frank Dobrzenski, Roman Kab, Barb Matthews, Mike Miller, Matt Mullin, Tom Robinette, Mike Swing, and Alfred Teoh for their REALLY GREAT contributions and Scripts for this book.

We would also like to thank Barb Matthews for her countless hours in the editing room and for her editing skills.

Cover photo taken by Mary Dunham.

All proceeds from the sale of this book will go to the Make-A-Wish Foundation.

Table of Contents

PREFACE

WHO WROTE THE WHAT SCRIPTS?

OATC, Oracle Applications and Technology Consulting, provides some of the most experienced, professional and competent consultants in the industry. We have sterling project references and experiences with many Oracle Applications and Technology projects. Below are some highlights of our expertise:

- Over 20 years experience with Oracle technology
- Over 20 years experience with Oracle EBS Applications
- Many Oracle EBS Application Implementations and Upgrades (MPL7→E-Buisiness9, E-Business10, E-Business11, E-Business12)
- Upgrade Assessments *(questionnaire and script oriented, low cost analysis and feedback)*
- CEMLI (*Customizations, Extensions, Modfications, Locations and Integrations/Intefaces*) Assessments
- Project Health Checks
- Custom Integration Projects
- Oracle EBS Applications Server Sizing and Recommendations
- Enhancing Oracle EBS Applications investment by utilizing more features and functionality of products purchased (a common problem)
- Superior Project Management and CRP Method
- Experienced Functional, Technical Developers and Database Adminsitrators
- Remote Oracle EBS Application Services (Functional, Technical Developers, and Database Administrators)
- Remote Oracle EBS Applications and Database Monitoring & Support
- Our clients tell us we are really good ☺

We – Bill Dunham and Michael Barone – decided to share our hard-won knowledge with the Oracle EBS user community by writing this book, and the *StreetSmarts®* series. ***What Scripts*** is the first in the series; it's a collection of very useful E-Business Suite scripts for your technical team members and super users. We have perfected these scripts at all of our client-sites, and they've proven very useful to us and our clients over many years on many Oracle E-Business Suite Releases and Versions.

WHAT ARE THE WHAT SCRIPTS?

Each of the Scripts in this book have been developed, tested and perfected on the following Computer Operating Systems:

AIX	HP/UX
Oracle Linux	Redhat Linux
Sun Solaris	SuSe Linux

Each of these Scripts will prompt the user for the necessary password and the Script will automatically screen-protect the password so the password is NOT visible on the screen. Additionally, each of these Scripts will monitor for the <CNTL><C> (cancel) or <CNTL><D> (delete) or <CNTL> <X> exit. So, if the Script-user cancels or stops the script, the password screen-protect settings are reversed and a normal terminal-setting resumes.

Each of these scripts MERELY SELECTS and DISPLAYS on the screen and simultaneously creates an identical file in the */tmp* directory so you can review these results anytime. The ***WhatScripts*** do NOT update any Database Tables, Rows, Columns nor Database Data. ***WhatScripts*** do NOT update any Configuration Files nor any Context Files nor any Setup Files.

MORE WHAT SCRIPTS TO COME!

We already have more ideas percolating, so stay tuned for updated versions of this book.

After reviewing our scripts you may scratch your head and say "*I have scripts just like that, or even better ones that I'd like to share*!" If you would like to contribute scripts to us for inclusion in the next version of this book, please email us at whatscripts@oatcinc.com. Please include your contact information, a brief description of the script, the script details and sample output. We will review and confirm that the script works as planned and provide feedback on its inclusion in the next version – we will certainly give credit where credit is due!

P.S. We're pretty busy doing our day jobs, so we can't make guarantees, but we do love a challenge so send those scripts along!

You can also download this book and the Scripts from this book at http://oatcinc.blogspot.com. Subscribe to our blog so you'll be the first to know when our next version of *StreetSmarts*® *What Scripts* is available.

CHAPTER 1 – "WHAT SCRIPTS"

WHAT SCRIPTS – WHAT ARE THEY ALL ABOUT?

The "what scripts" are a series of operating system level scripts that interrogate the Oracle E-Business Suiteinternal tables for information not easily obtained through other means. These scripts were created to provide information quickly, accurately, and in an easy to read format.

The "what scripts" are designed to assist System Administrators, Database Administrators, or really any IS/IT personnel looking for specific information such as what services are currently running to what users are logged in or what Concurrent Requests/Concurrent-Managers are busy or idle. There are a wide variety of scripts found within this book. Please review the table of contents and appendixes to find a "what" script that best meets your needs.

WHAT SCRIPTS (continued)

WHATS UP 11I/12.1 (M.BARONE)

- What E-Business Suite Services are UP?
- What E-Business Suite AppsTier and DBTier and Workflow Services are Available?

Use this Script to quickly determine which E-Business Suite DBTier and AppsTier Sevices are UP/DOWN When AppsTier/DBTier/Workflow Services are DOWN the Script shows "No" under the appropriate heading.

Example: AppsTier 11i/12.1 Services are UP. DBTier Services are UP.

```
           oratest.oatcinc.com Apps-11i/12.1 Survey

           A p p l i c a t i o n         D a t a b a s e
              S e r v i c e s            S e r v i c e s
              --  Apache --   App     App 11g 11g
Apps     Frm Svr Svr Svr JRE DB      Cnc DB  Ora  WF-Java WF-Java
SIDs     Svr iAS PLS 920 Svr Lnr     Mgr Lsr DB   Server  AgntLst
-------- --- --- --- --- --- ---     --- --- ---  ------- -------
oatc     Yes Yes Yes Yes Yes Yes     Yes Yes Yes  Running Running

            Current Activity
            ------------------------------
            Forms-Connections:           9
            ConcReqs Running:            2

            Daily Activity
            ------------------------------
            Web-AppsLocalLogin Today:   20
```

Example: AppsTier 11i/12.1 Services are DOWN. DBTier Services are UP.

```
             oratest.oatcinc.com Apps-11i/12.1 Survey

           A p p l i c a t i o n         D a t a b a s e
              S e r v i c e s            S e r v i c e s
              --  Apache --   App     App 11g 11g
Apps     Frm Svr Svr Svr JRE DB      Cnc DB  Ora  WF-Java WF-Java
SIDs     Svr iAS PLS 920 Svr Lnr     Mgr Lsr DB   Server  AgntLst
-------- --- --- --- --- --- ---     --- --- ---  ------- -------
oatc     No  No  No  No  No  No      No  Yes Yes  Running Running
```

WHAT SCRIPTS (continued)

WHATS UP 12.2 (T.BLANFORD)

- What E-Business Suite 12.2 Services are UP?
- What E-Business Suite 12.2 AppsTier and DBTier and Workflow Services are Available?

Use this Script to quickly determine which E-Business Suite 12.2 DBTier and AppsTier Sevices are UP/DOWN When AppsTier/DBTier/Workflow Services are DOWN the Script shows "No" under the appropriate heading.

Example: AppsTier 12.2 Services are UP. DBTier Services are UP.

```
                 oratest.oatcinc.com Apps-12.2 Survey

          A p p l i c a t i o n   ConcManager    D a t a b a s e
            S e r v i c e s        Services      S e r v i c e s
         -OA-Framework  Apache-    App  App      11g  11g
Apps     OAFM OA   Frm  Frm  App   DB   Cnc      DB   Ora  WF-Java WF-Java
SIDs     Svr  Core C4WL Svr  Lnr   Lnr  Mgr      Lsr  DB   Server  AgntLst
-------- ---- ---- ---- ---  ---   ---  ---      ---  ---  ------- -------
OATC122  Yes  Yes  Yes  Yes  Yes   Yes  Yes      Yes  Yes  Running Running
```

Example: AppsTier 12.2 Services are DOWN. DBTier Services are UP.

```
                   oratest.oatcinc.com Apps-12.2 Survey

          A p p l i c a t i o n   ConcManager    D a t a b a s e
            S e r v i c e s        Services      S e r v i c e s
         -OA-Framework  Apache-    App  App      11g  11g
Apps     OAFM OA   Frm  Frm  App   DB   Cnc      DB   Ora  WF-Java WF-Java
SIDs     Svr  Core C4WL Svr  Lnr   Lnr  Mgr      Lsr  DB   Server  AgntLst
-------- ---- ---- ---- ---  ---   ---  ---      ---  ---  ------- -------
OATC122  No   No   No   No   No    Yes  Yes      Yes  Yes  Running Running
```

WHAT SCRIPTS (continued)

WHOS UP (M.BARONE)

- Who is Connected to the E-Business Suite? Who is UP?
- Who has connected to the AppsTier (OAFramework/Forms)?

Since the E-Business Suite ICX (Internet Connections) are recorded in the ICX Tables, you can examine the ICX Connections that are current and/or historical. Additionally, the ICX history is available until the Concurrent Request: ***Purge Inactive Sessions*** is executed and the ICX activity is purged.

The Forms-Connections, on the other hand, are only available when they are active. So, when a Forms User disconnects, the **whosup** script will no longer show a User with an open Forms Session.

Example:

```
#------------------------------------------------------------------#
#- ICX Connections (whosup)                                        -#
#------------------------------------------------------------------#

09-JUL-12                    Apps ICX Connections
19:50:33                      Sorted by UserName
                                                             Last
                                                   ICX       ICX
UserName User Description Responsibility          Connect   Activity
-------- ---------------- ---------------------   --------- ---------
BARONEMI Barone, Michael  GL Superuser            09-JUL-12 09-JUL-12
                                                   18:45:58  19:43:05

SYSADMIN <HTTP Menu Only> System Administrator    09-JUL-12 09-JUL-12
                                                   18:23:34  18:23:34
```

```
#------------------------------------------------------------------#
#- Forms Connections (whosup)                                      -#
#------------------------------------------------------------------#

09-JUL-12                       Apps FormServer
19:50:33                        Sorted by UserName

                                                      AppsTier
                         Apps                         UNIX     Apps      DB&Form
                         Short                FormStart Server   Server     Server
UserNa FormName     Name  Responsibility  Time      ProcID   Name       AUDSID
------ ------------ ----- --------------- --------- -------- ------- ---------
BARONE Run Reports  FND   GL Superuser    09-JUL-12 26149062 oratest  86496124
                                          06:46:18
```

WHAT SCRIPTS (continued)

WHOS UP NODE (T.ROBINETTE)

- Who is Connected to the E-Business Suite? Who is UP?
- Who is Connected to the E-Business Suite on Which AppsTier Node?
- Who has connected to the AppsTier (OAFramework/Forms)?

Since the E-Business Suite ICX (Internet Connections) are recorded in the ICX Tables, you can examine the ICX Connections that are current and/or historical. Additionally, the ICX history is available until the Concurrent Request: ***Purge Inactive Sessions*** is executed and the ICX activity is purged.

The Forms-Connections, on the other hand, are only available when they are active. So, when a Forms User disconnects, the **whosup** script will no longer show a User with an open Forms Session.

Example:

```
#-----------------------------------------------------------------#
#- ICX Connections (whosupnode)                                  -#
#-----------------------------------------------------------------#

29-APR-15 PEBRM1 (rmco-chi-pap03.rmco.itciss.com) Apps ICX Connections
09:00:05                       Sorted by UserName
                                                                        Last
                                                      Node  ICX         ICX
UserName   User Description   Responsibility         Name  Connect     Activity
---------- ------------------ ---------------------- ----- ---------   ---------
BARONE     Michael Barone     GL Superuser           OATC1 29-APR-15   29-APR-15
                                                           09:47:41    08:54:31

BLANFORD   Tom Blanford       System Administrator   OATC1 29-APR-15   29-APR-15
                                                           08:47:41    08:54:31
```

```
#-----------------------------------------------------------------#
#- Forms Connections (whosup)                                    -#
#-----------------------------------------------------------------#

09-JUL-12                       Apps FormServer
19:50:33                       Sorted by UserName
                                                        AppsTier
                      Apps                              UNIX      Apps      DB&Form
                      Short                   FormStart Server    Server     Server
UserNa FormName       Name  Responsibility    Time      ProcID    Name       AUDSID
------ ------------   ----- --------------    --------- --------  -------  ---------
BARONE Run Reports    FND   GL Superuser      09-JUL-12 26149062  oratest   86496124
                                              06:46:18
```

WHAT SCRIPTS (continued)

WHOS UP DATE (M.BARONE)

- Who is Connected to the E-Business Suite? Who is UP Between Two Dates ?
- Who has connected to the AppsTier (OAFramework/Forms) FROM Dates ?

Since the E-Business Suite ICX (Internet Connections) are recorded in the ICX Tables, you can examine the ICX Connections that are current and/or historical. Additionally, the ICX history is available until the Concurrent Request: ***Purge Inactive Sessions*** is executed and the ICX activity is purged.

The Forms-Connections, on the other hand, are only available when they are active. So, when a Forms User disconnects, the **whosup_date** script will no longer show a User with an open Forms Session.

Example: Who Connected/Logged-In Between 01-SEP-15 and 09-SEP-15

```
#---------------------------------------------------------------#
#- ICX Connections (whosup_date)                               -#
#---------------------------------------------------------------#

10-SEP-15            PROD (rduoraprod) Apps ICX Connections
18:16:30                       Sorted by UserName
                                                                    Last
                                                          ICX       ICX
UserName   User Description   Responsibility              Connect   Activity
---------- ------------------ --------------------------- --------- ---------
M.BARONE   M.Barone    OATC   Cash Management Superuser   03-SEP-15 03-SEP-15
           Consultant                                     11:52:45  13:27:21

M.BARONE   M.Barone    OATC   RDU Payables Manager        09-SEP-15 09-SEP-15
           Consultant                                     16:29:38  19:47:06

M.BARONE   M.Barone    OATC   RDU Workflow User Web(New)  09-SEP-15 09-SEP-15
           Consultant                                     16:52:15  17:13:48


B.DUNHAM   B.DUNHAM    OATC   System Administrator        03-SEP-15 03-SEP-15
           Consultant                                     08:45:36  10:54:55

B.DUNHAM   B.Dunham    OATC   System Administrator        08-SEP-15 08-SEP-15
           Consultant                                     17:15:55  19:16:14


#---------------------------------------------------------------#
#- Forms Connections (whosup)                                  -#
#---------------------------------------------------------------#
```

WHAT SCRIPTS (continued)

WHAT CONC QUEUE (M.BARONE)

- What Concurrent Manager Queues are ACTIVE/RUNNING?
- What Concurrent Managers are ENABLED/DISABLED?
- What Concurrent Managers are Fully Loaded/Backlogged/Idle?

Use this Script to quickly examine/compare different E-Business Suite Environments and find the Concurrent Managers that are too-busy or under-utilized. Also this Script shows whether the Concurrent-Manager is in Debug-Mode or has a Diagnostic-Level.

Example:

```
28-MAY-14                    EBusiness Concurrent Queues                Page:    1
17:14:40                 whatconcqueue -- Sorted by Queue-Name

Concurrent           Concurrent Queue      Conc   Conc   Conc Conc     Conc
Queue                Queue      Enable    Queue  Queue  Queue Queue    Diag
Description          Name       Disable     Max Runing Target Node     Lvl
-------------------- ---------- -------- ----- ------ ------ ------- ----
C AQCART Service     C_AQCT_SVC Enabled       0      0      1
CRP Inquiry Manager  CRPINQMGR  Enabled       0      0      2          N
Conflict Resolution  FNDCRM     Enabled       1      1      1          N
Manager

Debug Service        Debug_Serv Enabled       0      0      1
                     ice

FastFormula          FFTM       Enabled       0      0      1
Transaction Manager

Human Resources      HRM        Enabled       3      3      3          N

INV Remote Procedure INVTMRPM   Enabled       0      0      4
Manager

Internal Manager     FNDICM     Enabled       1      1      0          N
Internal Monitor:    FNDIM_ORAT Enabled       0      0      0 ORATEST
ORATEST              TEST

Inventory Manager    INVMGR     Enabled       1      1      1          N
KBACE                KBACE      Enabled       5      5      5          N
Labor Distribution   LDMSTD     Enabled       3      3      3          N
.
.
.
Standard Manager     STANDARD   Enabled      20     20     20          N

Workflow Mailer      WFMGSMD    Enabled       0      0      1
Workflow Mailer      WFMLRSVC   Enabled       1      1      1
Service

Workflow Summary     WFMGSMS    Enabled       0      0      1
Mailer
```

WHAT SCRIPTS (continued)

WHATS RUNNING (M.BARONE)

- What Concurrent Requests are Currently Running?

The output includes **Submit-Time, Time-Waiting** and **Start-Time** in the Concurrent-Manager's Queue, etc.

Use these two Scripts to quickly determine the E-Business Suite Concurrent-Requests that are currently executing.

Example:

```
21-MAY-14      E-Business Concurrent Requests (Running)          Page:    1
09:50:39        whatsrunning -- Sorted by Start Time

                                   Unix
                                   Process  Submit    Wait Time Start
Concurrent Pgm Desc        ConcReq ID       Time      (Minutes) Time
------------------------- --------- -------- --------- --------- ---------
Retirement Report          16912471 10616872 28-JUN-14       .63 28-JUN-14
                                             09:46:58            09:47:36

Calculate and update       16912455 27721860 28-JUN-14       .37 28-JUN-14
benefit eligibility                           09:25:17            09:25:39
```

WHATS RUNNING DETAILS (M.BARONE)

- What Concurrent Requests are Currently Running? – ConcMgrTier Details.

Example:

```
12-MAY-14         E-Business Concurrent Requests (Detail)          Page:    1
18:03:58          whatrunningdetail -- Sorted by Start Time

                                         Unix
                                         Process  Concurrent         Start
Concurrent Req      ConcReq Requestor   ID       Arguments          Time
---------------- --------- ----------- -------- ------------------ ---------
Gather Schema     17587173  MBARONE     21037104 APPLSYS, 30        12-MAY-12
Statistics                                                          12:04:00
```

WHAT SCRIPTS (continued)

WHAT CONC DAILY (M.BARONE)

- What Concurrent Requests Executed/Completed Today ?

The output includes Concurrent Program/Report Name, Average Run-Time and Number of Executions.

Use this Script to quickly summarize and report on the E-Business Suite Concurrent-Requests that completed in the past day. Additionally, this Script shows the Average-Execution-Time and the Number of times the Concurrent-Request was executed in the past day.

Example:

```
21-MAY-14      E-Business Concurrent Requests (Daily Summary)       Page:    1
17:55:18                DBA ConcMgr Summary Report

                         Concurrent                                Avg.     Number
                         Program                               Run-Time         of
Concurrent Description   Name                                 (Minutes) Executions
------------------------ ----------------------------- --------- ----------
Aging-7 Bucket Report    Aging - 7 Buckets Report             82.13          1
                         Open Account Balances Data           26.59         11
                         Manager Worker Process

                         Open Account Balances Data           15.87         20
                         Manager

                         Open Account Balances Listing         9.82          1
Gather Table Statis      Gather Table Statistics               9.33          4
Request Set Master Progr Report Set                            2.91          4
RF Employee Benefit      RF OAB Benefit Election               2.56          3
Request Set Stage Master Request Set Stage                     2.40          4
Program

Report for the Accountin Create Accounting                     2.30          4
Program

Child thread for the     Accounting Program                    1.68          4
Accounting Program

Purges Concurrent reques Purge Concurrent Request               .85          2
and/or Concurrent Manage and/or Manager Data
data and log/output file

.
.
.

                                                                   ----------
                                                                          820
```

WHAT SCRIPTS (continued)

WHAT CONC SUMMARY (M.BARONE)

- What Concurrent Requests Executed/Completed in the Past Week (7 Days)?

The output includes Concurrent Program/Report Name, Average Run-Time and Number of Executions.

Use this Script to quickly summarize and report on the E-Business Suite Concurrent-Requests that completed in the past week (7-Days). Additionally, this Script shows the Average-Execution-Time and the Number of times the Concurrent-Request was executed in the past week (7-Days).

Example:

```
21-MAY-14    E-Business Concurrent Requests (Weekly Summary)      Page:    1
20:15:36          whatconcsummary --  DBA ConcMgr Summary Report

                              Concurrent                     Avg.     Number
                              Program                    Run-Time        of
Concurrent Pgm Description    Name                      (Minutes) Executions
----------------------------- ---------------------- --------- ----------
Application Accounting        Validate Application       33.64          2
Definition Validation Report  Accounting Definitions

                              Import Application           .91          6
                              Accounting Definitions

User Responsibility Report    Active Users                 .43          1
OAM Applications Dashboard    OAM Applications Dashboard   .13        937
Collection                    Collection

                              Upload Application           .11          6
                              Accounting Definitions

DQM Serial Sync Index         DQM Serial Sync Index Pgm    .01          3
Program for online flow

.
.
.

                                                                ----------
                                                                      1520
```

WHAT SCRIPTS (continued)

WHAT CONC SUMMARY PARMS (M.BARONE)

- What Concurrent Requests + Parameters Completed in the Past Week ?

The output includes Concurrent Program/Report Name, Parameters & Run-Time.

Use this Script to quickly summarize and report on the E-Business Suite Concurrent-Requests that completed in the past week (7-Days). Additionally, this Script shows the Concurrent-Request-Arguments and the Execution-Time.

Example:

```
03-SEP-13       E-Business Concurrent Requests (Weekly Summary)     Page:    1
13:58:58                DBA ConcMgr + Parameters Report
                                                                      Run-Time
Concurrent Pgm Description      Concurrent Arguments                  (Minutes)
---------------------------- ------------------------------------ --------
Accounts Payable Trial Bala 200, 21, AP_200_2, Payables,                 3.40
nce                         1950/01/01 00:00:00, 2013/06/30
                            00:00:00, , 101, , , YEAR_TO_DATE, Y,
                            , , , , , N, No, S, Summary

Import Application Account  200, DEFAULT,                                  .70
Ing Definitions             /d121/app/121/appl/xla/12.0.0/
                                patch/115/import/US/xlaap.ldt, N, , Y,
                                MERGE, Y, ,


Gather Schema Statistics    PO, 40, , NOBACKUP, , LASTRUN, GATHER,      42.32
Gather Schema Statistics    , Y
```

WHAT CONC MONTHLY (M.BARONE)

- What Concurrent Requests Executed/Completed This Month ?

The output includes Concurrent Program/Report Name, Average Run-Time and Number of Executions.

Use this Script to quickly summarize and report on the E-Business Suite Concurrent-Requests that completed in the past Month (30 Days. Additionally, this Script shows the Average-Execution-Time and the Number of times the Concurrent-Request was executed in the past 30 Days.

Example:

```
21-MAY-14      E-Business Concurrent Requests (Monthly Summary)     Page:    1
17:55:18                DBA ConcMgr Summary Report

                         Concurrent                          Avg.      Number
                         Program                         Run-Time          of
Concurrent Description   Name                           (Minutes) Executions
------------------------ ----------------------------- --------- ----------
Aging- 7 Bucket Report   Aging - 7 Buckets Report          82.13          1
                         Open Account Balances Data        26.59         11
                         Manager Worker Process

                         Open Account Balances Data        15.87         20
                         Manager

                         Open Account Balances Listing      9.82          1
Gather Table Statis      Gather Table Statistics            9.33          4
Request Set Master Progr Report Set                         2.91          4
RF Employee Benefit      RF OAB Benefit Election            2.56          3
Request Set Stage Master Request Set Stage                  2.40          4
Program

Report for the Accountin Create Accounting                  2.30          4
Program

Child thread for the     Accounting Program                 1.68          4
Accounting Program

Purges Concurrent reques Purge Concurrent Request            .85          2
and/or Concurrent Manage and/or Manager Data
data and log/output file

.
.
.

                                                                  ----------
                                                                        7580
```

WHAT SCRIPTS (continued)
WHAT CONC MGRS (F.BENDER)

- What Conc Mgrs counts the completed ConcReq in each Manager ?
- What Conc Mgrs summarizes the ConcMgr activity for the past 30 days.

The output includes Concurrent Manager Name and Number of ConcRequests.

Use this Script to quickly summarize and report on the E-Business Suite Concurrent-Managers Concurrent-Requests that completed in the past Month (30 Days. Additionally, this Script can be used to show when a Custom Concurent Manager is seldom-used or no-longer-used.

Example:

```
11-AUG-15       E-Business Concurrent Requests (ConcMgr Summary)
21:53:12                   DBA ConcMgr Summary Report

                                                Number
                                                    of
Concurrent Pgm Description              ConcRequests
------------------------------------ ------------
OATCinc: CloseDiscrete Jobs                       79
OATCinc: CloseWorkOrderJobs                       66
OATCinc: Critical Jobs                            55
OATCinc: Critical Jobs - Standby                   4
OATCinc: FNDMLSUB                                 20
OATCinc: Fast Jobs                             17344
OATCinc: Fast Jobs - Standby                    3596
OATCinc: High Workload                          1717
OATCinc: HighWorkload - Standby                  362
OATCinc: Interface Supplier Cst                    4
OATCinc: Standard                               6007
OATCinc: Standard - Standby                     1036
OATCinc: XML                                     164
Inventory Manager                                 5455
```

WHAT SCRIPTS (continued)

WHAT CONC SCHEDULE (M.BARONE)

- What Concurrent Requests are Scheduled ?

The output includes Concurrent Program/ReqID, Parameters & Schedule-Type.

Use this Script to quickly report on the E-Business Suite Concurrent-Requests that are Scheduled to execute and repeat. Additionally, this Script shows the current-pending Concurrent-Request-ID, the Concurrent-Arguments, the Schedule (repeat) type and the Schedule-Information.

Example:

```
03-MAY-14   E-Business Scheduled Concurrent Requests (Summary)      Page:    1
16:33:17             DBA Scheduled ConcRequests Report

Concurrent         ConcReq   Concurrent Hold Schedule Schedule         Schedule
Pgm Description    ID Number Arguments  Flag Type     Desc             Info
----------------  --------- ---------- ---- -------- ---------------- --------
Purge Concurrent   16942714 REQUEST,   N    Periodic Repeat Every 7   7:D:S
Request and/or              Age, 30, ,               days from the s
Manager Data                , , , , ,                tart of the pri
                            , , Y, Y                 or run
```

WHAT SCRIPTS (continued)

WHAT FREESPACE (S.BOMMAREDDY)

- What is the Database Freespace: Tablespace, Fragments, Percent-Used ?

Use this Script to quickly summarize the size of each Databse Tablespace and the size of the Total Database: Total Space, Used Space, Free Space and Percent-Used.

Example:

```
19-MAY-14     oatc (oratest.oatcinc.com) EBusiness Database Report
11:07:18        whatfreespace --  EBusiness Database Freespace
```

TableSpace	Num DBFs	Free Frag	Total Space(Kb)	Used Space(Kb)	Free Space(Kb)	Pct Used
APPS_TS_SUMMARY	1	1	204,800	128	204,672	0
APPS_TRANSACTION_TABLES	1	1	2,097,152	128	2,097,024	0
APPS_TS_TOOLS	2	2	1,253,376	256	1,253,120	0
APPS_TS_INTERFACE	1	1	204,800	128	204,672	0
APPS_UNCLASSIFIED	1	1	204,800	128	204,672	0
INTERIM	1	1	204,800	128	204,672	0
APPS_TRANSACTION_INDEXES	1	1	921,600	128	921,472	0
APPS_TS_SEED	2	2	409,600	256	409,344	0
APPS_TS_NOLOGGING	1	1	51,200	640	50,560	1
PORTAL	1	1	5,120	80	5,040	2
OWAPUB	1	1	5,120	80	5,040	2
USERS	1	1	5,120	80	5,040	2
APPS_TS_QUEUES	2	1	2,168,832	162,432	2,006,400	7
APPS_NOLOGGING	2	1	2,590,720	193,792	2,396,928	7
TOOLS	1	3	51,200	8,360	42,840	16
APPS_INTERFACE	2	62	2,097,152	819,968	1,277,184	39
APPS_SUMMARY	2	4	2,609,152	1,232,768	1,376,384	47
APPS_TS_ARCHIVE	3	6	9,601,024	5,486,592	4,114,432	57
CTXSYS	1	24	20,480	15,456	5,024	75
SYSTEM	7	164	14,336,000	10,761,296	3,574,704	75
APPS_REFERENCE	2	1	3,145,728	2,436,224	709,504	77
OLAPSYS	1	1	12,288	10,008	2,280	81
APPS_TS_MEDIA	3	3	7,379,328	6,669,568	709,760	90
APPS_UNDOTS1	2	10	4,096,000	3,883,008	212,992	95
APPS_TS_TX_IDX	8	4	13,942,912	13,278,848	664,064	95
SYSAUX	2	47	6,556,672	6,200,320	356,352	95
APPS_TS_TX_DATA	9	14	22,158,592	21,104,000	1,054,592	95
	62	360	96,343,808	72,265,824	24,077,984	

WHAT SCRIPTS (continued)

WHAT FREESPACE GRAPH (M.BARONE)

- What is the Database Freespace: Tablespace, Fragments, Percent-Used ?

Use this Script to quickly summarize the size of each Databse Tablespace and the size of the Total Database: Total Space, Used Space, Free Space and Percent-Used in Graph format

Example:

```
19-May-14          oratest.oatcinc.com) E-Business Freespace Graph
11:28:46                     eBusiness Suite

                                                                  Used
Tablespace              Used      Free      Max      Max     Free Percent
Name               Space(Mb) Space(Mb) Size(Mb) Free(Mb)  Percent Graph
------------------ --------- --------- -------- -------- -------- -----------
APPS_TS_ARCHIVE         7000       761     7000      761       10  XXXXXXXXX-
APPS_TS_INTERFACE       6000      1315     6000     1315       21  XXXXXXXX--
APPS_TS_MEDIA         146432      3831   146432     3831        2  XXXXXXXXXX
APPS_TS_NOLOGGING       1500       945     1500      945       63  XXXX------
APPS_TS_QUEUES          4000       742     4000      742       18  XXXXXXXX--
APPS_TS_SEED            3000       173     3000      173        5  XXXXXXXXX-
APPS_TS_SUMMARY         4000       213     4000      213        5  XXXXXXXXX-
APPS_TS_TOOLS            500       499      500      499       99  ----------
APPS_TS_TX_DATA       410624      5913   410624     5913        1  XXXXXXXXXX
APPS_TS_TX_DATA2        6720      6551     6720     6551       97  ----------
APPS_TS_TX_IDX        389680      3529   389680     3529        0  XXXXXXXXXX
APPS_TS_TX_IDX2            5         4        5        4       80  XX--------
APPS_UNDOTS1           40000     21564    40000    21564       53  XXXXX-----
APPS_UNDOTS2            5120      5117     5120     5117       99  ----------
CTXSYS                   500       465      500      465       93  X---------
DBA_TOOLS               1000       547     1000      547       54  XXXXX-----
.
.
.
SYSAUX                 10240      5143    10240     5143       50  XXXXX-----
SYSTEM                 19637      2745    36768    19876       54  XXXXX-----
                   --------- --------- -------- --------
                     1246554     86159  1328219   167824
```

WHAT SCRIPTS (continued)

WHAT TEMP FILES (M.Barone)

- What Database TEMP Files are included in the E-Business Suite Database?

Use this Script to quickly list the E-Business Suite Database TEMP-Files. Additionally, this Script will also list those Database TEMP-Files that are in AutoExtend-Mode and the Maximum AutoExtend File-Size.

Example:

```
12-MAY-14                   Tablespace TEMP DBA Report               Page:    1
14:06:42                    Oracle Tablespace/File Name
                                                                        Auto
                                                                      Extend
                                                      Tablespace        Size Auto
Tablespace         Temp FileName                      Size(Bytes)    (Bytes) Extend
------------------ ------------------------------ ------------ -------- ------
TEMP               /d150/oradata/OATC/temp1.dbf   18874368000          0 NO
TEMP               /d150/oradata/OATC/temp2.dbf       5242880          0 NO
```

WHAT SCRIPTS (continued)

WHAT FNDNODE (M.BARONE)

- What are the FND_NODES Servers and Server Assignments?

Use this Script to quickly show the E-Business Suite Nodes/Servers used by the E-Business Suite Environment.

Example: **Single-Node Installation**

```
21-MAY-14          oatc (oratest.oatcinc.com) Apps FND_NODES
18:18:04          EBusiness AdminTier/ConcTier/FormTier/WebTier

                                                           Admn Conc Form Web
Node Name         Host Name Virtual Addr Server Address Srvr Srvr Srvr Srvr
--------------- --------- ------------ -------------- ---- ---- ---- ----
AUTHENTICATION                         *                N    N    N    N
ORATEST                     oratest      126.4.4.171    Y    Y    Y    Y
```

Example: **Multi-Node Installation**

```
21-MAY-14          oatc (oratest.oatcinc.com) Apps FND_NODES
20:05:18          EBusiness AdminTier/ConcTier/FormTier/WebTier

                                                           Admn Conc Form Web
Node Name         Host Name Virtual Addr Server Address Srvr Srvr Srvr Srvr
--------------- --------- ------------ -------------- ---- ---- ---- ----
AUTHENTICATION                         *                N    N    N    N
ORATESTA        oratesta                 10.1.10.110    Y    Y    Y    Y
ORATESTD        oratestd    oratestd                    N    N    N    N
```

WHAT SCRIPTS (continued)

WHAT APPS (M.BARONE)

- What E-Business Suite Products Use Which Tablespaces (Default and Temp)?
- What E-Business Suite Products correlate to Application-Schema-ID?
- What E-Business Suite Products correlate to Oracle-Schema-ID?

Use this Script to quickly examine/compare different E-Business Suite Environments and find the Application-Short-Name and the corresponding Application-Base-Path and DEFAULT Tablespace and TEMP Tablespace.

Example:

```
#--------------------------------------------------------------#
#- What Apps Products/Default and TempTablespace (whatapps)   -#
#--------------------------------------------------------------#

11-JUN-14          OATC (oratest) Apps Details Tablespace
14:39:50           whatspps --  E-Business Apps Product Tablespace

Oracle        App   App      FND      App FND           DBA             DBA
  User    APP Short Base     Oracle   Grp Read DBA Default              Temp
    ID     ID Name  Path     UserNm   No. Only Use Tablespace           Tblsp
------ ------ ----- -------- ------- ---- ---- --- ---------------- ------
   867    867 AHL   AHL_TOP  AHL        1 A    Yes APPS_TS_TX_DATA  TEMP
   601    601 AK    AK_TOP   AK         0 A    Yes APPS_TS_TX_DATA  TEMP
   160    160 ALR   ALR_TOP  ALR        0 A    Yes APPS_TS_TX_DATA  TEMP
   530    530 AMS   AMS_TOP  AMS        1 A    Yes APPS_TS_TX_DATA  TEMP
   520    520 AMV   AMV_TOP  AMV        1 A    Yes APPS_TS_TX_DATA  TEMP
   242    242 AMW   AMW_TOP  AMW        0 A    Yes APPS_TS_TX_DATA  TEMP
   222    222 AR    AR_TOP   AR         1 A    Yes APPS_TS_TX_DATA  TEMP
     .
     .
     .

 20066                      EDWREP           X    No  Unknown          Unknown
 20065                      ODM              X    No  Unknown          Unknown
 20069                      PORTAL30         X    No  Unknown          Unknown
 20067                      CTXSYS           X    Yes CTXSYS           TEMP
```

WHAT SCRIPTS (continued)

WHAT USER ACTIVITY (F.BENDER)

- What E-Business Suite Users have Connected in the Past 30/60/90 Days?
- What E-Business Suite User Location?
- What E-Business Suite User Supervisor Name?

Use this Script to quickly find the E-Business Suite Users that have connected and used the E-Business Suite over the past 30-days, 60-days and 90-days.

Example:

```
#----------------------------------------------------------------#
#- What Apps Users Connections: 30-Days, 60-Days and 90-Days   -#
#----------------------------------------------------------------#

01-APR-15     E-Business Suite User Activity - 30/60/90 Days         Page:   1
04:13:46         whatuser_activity -- 30/60/90 Days

                                                                User User User
User     User     User     User     Start     End      Last      Last Last Last
Location Supervis EMP-Name Name     Date       Date    LogOn     30Da 60Da 90Da
-------- -------- -------- -------- --------- -------- --------- ---- ---- ----
Raleigh  Dunham,  Mary     MDUNHAM  06-MAY-94          01-APR-15    Y    Y    Y
- 0100   William  Dunham

Raleigh  Dunham,  Michael  MBARONE  03-MAY-96          01-APR-15    Y    Y    Y
- 0100   William  Barone
```

WHAT SCRIPTS (continued)

WHAT USER CONNECT (A.TEOH)

- What E-Business Suite Users have Connected-Responsibility?
- What E-Business Suite User Language?
- What E-Business Suite User Total Connections?

Use this Script to quickly find the E-Business Suite Users that have connected and used the E-Business Suite and the Responsibility they used.

Example:

```
#-------------------------------------------------------------#
#- What Apps Users Connections                                -#
#-------------------------------------------------------------#

01-APR-15          E-Business Suite User Connections                    Page:    1
04:39:58         whatuser_connect - User-Responsibility

                                         Responsibility                           Total
Application Name     Responsibility Name  Description          Language Connects
-------------------- -------------------- -------------------- -------- --------
Application Object L Application Develope Application Object L US           4024
Ibrary               r                    ibrary Application D
                                          eveloper

Application Object L Functional Administr                      US             11
Ibrary               ator

.
.
.

System Administratio System Administrator Application Object L US             44
N                                         ibrary System Admins
                                          Trator


.
.
.
```

WHAT SCRIPTS (continued)

WHAT PAY ACTION PARAMETERS (M.BARONE)

- What E-Business Suite HRMS PAY (Payroll) Action Parameters ?

Use this Script to quickly examine/compare different E-Business Suite Environments and find the HRMS Payroll PAY_ACTION_PARAMETERS used for HRMS Payroll Processing.

Example:

```
#-----------------------------------------------------------------#
#- What HRMS PAY Action Parameters (whatpayactionparameters)    -#
#-----------------------------------------------------------------#


11-JUN-14          OATC (oratest) DBA Report                    Page:    1
                   Oracle PAY_ACTION_PARAMETERS
                     whatpayactionparameters

Parameter
Name                 Parameter Value
-------------------- ------------------------------------------------------------
BAL_BUFFER_SIZE      500
CHUNK_SIZE           20
DBC_FILE             /d121/app/appl/fnd/11.5.0/secure/OATCprod.dbc

EE_BUFFER_SIZE       500
HR_DM_DEBUG_LOG      SUMM:FAIL
HR_DM_DEBUG_PIPE     none
LAT_BAL_CHECK_MODE   B
LOW_VOLUME           N
PRINTER_MEM_SIZE     32768
PRINT_FILES          N
PROCESS_TIMEOUT      90
RANGE_PERSON_ID      Y
RRV_BUFFER_SIZE      500
RR_BUFFER_SIZE       500
RUN_XDO              N
TAX_DATA             /d01/121/appl/pay/12.0.0/vendor/quantum/data
TAX_LIBRARIES        /d01/121/appl/pay/12.0.0/vendor/quantum/lib
THREADS              12
TRACE                N
TRANSGL_THREAD       Y
```

CHAPTER 2 – "WHAT ADOP (ONLINE PATCHING)"

WHAT ADOP (ONLINE PATCHING) SCRIPTS – WHAT ARE THEY ALL ABOUT?

The "what adop (OnLine Patching scripts" are a series of operating system level scripts that interrogate the Oracle E-Business Suite internal tables for information not easily obtained through other means. These scripts were created to provide information quickly, accurately, and in an easy to read format.

The "what adop (OnLine Patching) scripts" are designed to assist System Administrators, Database Administrators, or really any IS/IT personnel looking for specific information such as what-adop-valid-nodes and what-edition, etc. . There are a wide variety of scripts found within this book. Please review the table of contents and appendixes to find a "what" script that best meets your needs.

WHAT ADOP (OnLine Patching) SCRIPTS (continued)

WHAT ADOP NODE (TOM BLANFORD)

- What ADOP (OnLine Patching) Nodes are Valid?

Use this Script to quickly displays the ADOP (OnLine Patching) Valid Nodes. If the adop (OnLine Patching) fails, there is a chance that the ADOP_VALID_NODES will NOT be correct. So, this what adop node script will help diagnose any ADOP Valid Nodes issues.

Example:

```
#------------------------------------------------------------------#
#- What (whatadopnode)                          ADOP_VALID_NODES -#
#------------------------------------------------------------------#

14-MAY-15            OATCinc (oatcinc1.oatcinc.com)          Page:    1
20:35:22              E-Business ADOP Valid Nodes

Node Name                      Context Name                   ADZD_Name
------------------------------ ------------------------------ --------------
oatcinc1-app01                 OATCPROD_oatcinc1-app01        V_20150514_0319
oatcinc1-app01                 OATCPROD_oatcinc1-app01        V_20150427_1832

oatcinc1-app01                 OATCPROD_oatcinc1-app02        V_20150514_0319
oatcinc1-app01                 OATCPROD_oatcinc1-app02        V_20150427_1832

oatcinc1-app01                 OATCPROD_oatcinc1-app03        V_20150427_1832
oatcinc1-app01                 OATCPROD_oatcinc1-app03        V_20150514_0319

oatcinc1-app01                 OATCPROD_oatcinc1-pdb01        V_20150514_0319
oatcinc1-app01                 OATCPROD_oatcinc1-pdb01        V_20150427_1832
```

CHAPTER 3 – "WHAT DEEP-DIVE SCRIPTS"

WHAT DEEP DIVE SCRIPTS – WHAT ARE THEY ALL ABOUT?

The "what deep dive scripts" are a series of operating system level scripts that interrogate the Oracle E-Business Suiteinternal tables for information not easily obtained through other means. These scripts were created to provide information quickly, accurately, and in an easy to read format.

The "what deep dive scripts" are designed to assist System Administrators, Database Administrators, or really any IS/IT personnel looking for specific information such as what-apps-versions and what-products-are-installed. There are a wide variety of scripts found within this book. Please review the table of contents and appendixes to find a "what" script that best meets your needs.

WHAT DEEP-DIVE SCRIPTS (continued)

WHAT OBJECTS (F.DOBRZENSKI)

- What Database/Data Dictionary Objects belong to What Schema/Owner?

Use this Script to quickly compare different Environments and find missing objects (Tables, Indexes, Triggers, Views, Synonyms, Sequences, DBLinks, Triggers, Functions, Procedures, Packages and Java-Classes).

Example:

```
#-------------------------------------------------------------------#
#- What DataDictionary Objects (whatobjects)                       -#
#-------------------------------------------------------------------#
```

OATC (oratest) Apps DataDictionary
EBusiness DataDictionary Schema Object Count

OWNER	TOTAL	CLU	TABLE	TABLE PART	INDEX	INDEX PART	VIEW	SYN	SEQ	DB LNK	TRIG	FUNC PROC	PACK	PACK BODY	JAVA CLASS
ABM	88		42		46										
AHL	569		149		306				110				2	2	
AK	192		59		116				13				2	2	
ALR	128		32		76				16				2	2	
AMDISCO	495		94		387		8		2			4			
AMS	1527		365		887				262				2	2	
AMV	184		40		98		2	6	27				2	2	
AMW	503		176		216				107				2	2	
AP	1176		337	64	628				139				2	2	
APPLSYS	3431		950	120	1413	294	108	6	234				2	2	
APPLSYSPUB	18							18							
APPQOSSYS	5		4					1							
APPS	169298		1378	129	2258	159	25469	38144	47	3	4248	358	47397	46338	367
AR	2640		697	159	1352	43	8	6	338				2	2	
ASF	10		2		3				1				2	2	
ASG	161		62		71				20				2	2	
ASL	43		14		20				3				2	2	

WHAT DEEP-DIVE SCRIPTS (continued)

WHAT ATG (M.BARONE)

- What E-Business Suite Application Technology Group (ATG) Patches have been applied?

Use this Script to quickly report on the E-Business Suite Application Technology Group (ATG) applied Patches and Versions.

This Script will change each time the Oracle ATG Team releases a new ATG Patch. So, please download the latest version of this Script from: http://oatcinc.blogspot.com/

Example:

```
#----------------------------------------------------------------#
#- What Application Technology Group (ATG) Patches (whatatg)   -#
#----------------------------------------------------------------#

28-MAY-14               OATC (oratest) Apps ATG Version
16:54:21          EBusiness 12 ATG (Application Technology Group)

RELEASE_NAME
--------------------------------------------------
12.1.3



28-MAY-14               OATC (oratest) Apps ATG Version
16:54:21          EBusiness 12 ATG (Application Technology Group)

Patch                                                                    Patch
Number   Date        Patch Description                                   Name
-------- ----------- --------------------------------------------------- -------
5907545  01-MAY-2014 R12.ATG_PF.A.DELTA.1                                R12
5917344  01-MAY-2014 R12.ATG_PF.A.DELTA.2                                R12
6077669  01-MAY-2014 R12.ATG_PF.A.DELTA.3                                R12
6241631  31-DEC-2010 11i.ATG_PF.H.RUP7                                   11i
6272680  01-MAY-2014 R12.ATG_PF.A.DELTA.4                                R12
6435000  01-MAY-2014 12.0.4 Release Update Pack (RUP4)                   R12
6678700  01-MAY-2014 12.1.1 Cumulative Update                            R12
7303030  01-MAY-2014 12.1.1 Cumulative Update                            R12
7303033  14-MAY-2014 12.1.2 Cumulative Update                            R12
7651091  14-MAY-2014 R12.ATG_PF.B.DELTA.2                                R12
8919491  14-MAY-2014 R12.ATG_PF.B.DELTA.3                                R12
9239090  14-MAY-2014 12.1.3 Cumulative Update                            R12
```

WHAT DEEP-DIVE SCRIPTS (continued)

WHAT VERSION (TOM ROBINETTE)

- What E-Business Suite Application Versions and Family-Packs and Maintenance Packs have been applied to each of the E-Business Suite Products?

Use this Script to quickly report on the E-Business Suite Application-Products. Additionally, this Script will show the Application-Product-Status (Installed, , Inactive), the Application-Version, the Application Patch Level and the Application-Product Last Update Date.

Example:

```
#----------------------------------------------------------------#
#- Oracle Apps Product Version                   (whatversion) -#
#----------------------------------------------------------------#

28-MAY-14          OATC (oratest) EBusiness Product Version
16:58:13         whatversion -- EBusiness Product Patch-Levels

App                                                App
Short                           App       App      Patch        Update
Name     Description            Status    Version  Level        Date
-------- ---------------------- --------- -------- ------------ -----------
AD       Applications DBA       Shared    12.0.0   R12.AD.B.3   01-May-2014
AHL      Complex Maintenance an Inactive  12.0.0   R12.AHL.B.3  01-May-2014
         d Overhaul

AK       Common Modules-AK      Installed 12.0.0   R12.AK.B.3   01-May-2014
ALR      Alert                  Installed 12.0.0   R12.ALR.B.3  01-May-2014
AME      Approvals Management   Inactive  12.0.0   R12.AME.B.5  01-May-2014
AMS      Marketing              Shared    12.0.0   R12.AMS.B.3  12-May-2014
AMV      Marketing Encyclopedia Shared    12.0.0   R12.AMV.B.3  01-May-2014
AMW      Internal Controls Mgr  Inactive  12.0.0   R12.AMW.B.3  01-May-2014
.
.
.
XDO      XML Publisher          Installed 12.0.0   R12.XDO.B.3  01-MAY-2014
XDP      Provisioning           Inactive  12.0.0   R12.XDP.B.3  01-MAY-2014
XLA      Subledger Accounting   Shared    12.0.0   R12.XLA.B.3  01-MAY-2014
XLE      Legal Entity Config    Inactive  12.0.0   R12.XLE.B.3  01-MAY-2014
XNB      Oracle Telecommunicatns Inactive 12.0.0   R12.XNB.B.3  01-MAY-2014
         ling Integrator

XNP      Number Portability     Inactive  12.0.0   R12.XNP.B.3  01-MAY-2014
XTR      Treasury               Inactive  12.0.0   R12.XTR.B.3  01-MAY-2014
ZFA      Financial Analyzer     Inactive  12.0.0   -- Not Avai  24-Apr-2007
                                                   lable --

ZPB      Enterprise Planning and Inactive 12.0.0   R12.ZPB.B.3  01-MAY-2014
         Budgeting

ZSA      Sales Analyzer         Inactive  12.0.0   -- Not Avai  24-Apr-2007
                                                   lable --

ZX       E-Business Tax         Inactive  12.0.0   R12.ZX.B.3   01-MAY-2014
```

WHAT DEEP-DIVE SCRIPTS (continued)

WHAT PRODUCT INFO (B.MATTHEWS)

- What E-Business Suite Application Products are Installed/Shared/Inactive or Pseudo?

Use this Script to quickly report on the E-Business Suite Application-Products. and the Application-Product Installed-Status (Installed, Shared, Inactive and Pseudo).

Example:

```
#-----------------------------------------------------------------#
#- What (whatproductinfo)                                        -#
#-----------------------------------------------------------------#

                OATC (oratest) Apps Product Information
                  Whatproductinfo  --  EBusiness Suite

App
Short                                                  Install
Name     Application  Name                             Status
-------- ------------------------------------------------ -------------
AD       Applications DBA                              Shared
ADO      Oracle Applications Patch Wizard              Pseudo
ADX      Rapid Install                                 Pseudo
AHL      Complex Maintenance Repair and Overhaul       Inactive
AK       Common Modules-AK                             Installed
ALR      Alert                                         Installed
AME      Approvals Management                          Inactive
AML      Leads Management                              Pseudo
AMS      Marketing                                     Shared
AMV      Marketing Encyclopedia System                 Shared
.
.
.
XDO      XML Publisher                                 Installed
XDP      Provisioning                                  Inactive
XLA      Subledger Accounting                          Shared
XLE      Legal Entity Configurator                     Inactive
XLH      Financial Services Accounting Hub             Pseudo
XNB      Oracle Telecommunications Billing Integrator  Inactive
XNP      Number Portability                            Inactive
XTR      Treasury                                      Inactive
ZFA      Financial Analyzer                            Inactive
ZPB      Enterprise Planning and Budgeting             Inactive
ZSA      Sales Analyzer                                Inactive
ZX       E-Business Tax                                Inactive
```

WHAT DEEP-DIVE SCRIPTS (continued)

WHATS INSTALLED (B.MATTHEWS)

- What E-Business Suite Application Products are Installed/Not-Installed/Shared?

Use this Script to also report on the E-Business Suite Application-Products. and the Application-Product Installed-Status (Installed, Not-Installed and Shared).

Example:

```
#-----------------------------------------------------------------#
#- What (whatinstalled)                                          -#
#-----------------------------------------------------------------#

10-JUN-14           OATC (oratest) Apps Installed Products
21:50:21              whatinstalled  --  EBusiness Suite

App
Short                                                         Install
Name     Application  Name                                    Status
-------- ------------------------------------------------    --------------
AD       Applications DBA                                     Shared
AHL      Complex Maintenance Repair and Overhaul              Not Installed
AK       Common Modules-AK                                    Installed
ALR      Alert                                                Installed
AME      Approvals Management                                 Not Installed
AMS      Marketing                                            Shared
AMV      Marketing Encyclopedia System                        Shared
AMW      Internal Controls Manager                            Not Installed
AR       Receivables                                          Installed
AS       Sales Foundation                                     Installed
ASF      Sales Online                                         Not Installed
ASG      CRM Gateway for Mobile Devices                       Not Installed
.
.
.
XDO      XML Publisher                                        Installed
XDP      Provisioning                                         Not Installed
XLA      Subledger Accounting                                 Shared
XLE      Legal Entity Configurator                            Not Installed
XNB      Oracle Telecommunications Billing Integrator         Not Installed
XNP      Number Portability                                   Not Installed
XTR      Treasury                                             Not Installed
ZFA      Financial Analyzer                                   Not Installed
ZPB      Enterprise Planning and Budgeting                    Not Installed
ZSA      Sales Analyzer                                       Not Installed
ZX       E-Business Tax                                       Not Installed
```

WHAT DEEP-DIVE SCRIPTS (continued)

WHAT FORMSERVER (M.MILLER)

- What is the E-Business Suite AppsTier Form-Server Version ?

Use this Script to quickly report on the E-Business Suite Form-Server Version.

Example:

```
#---------------------------------------------------------#
# whatformserver:   Oracle AppsTier Forms Server Version #
#---------------------------------------------------------#

Forms 10.1 (Form Compiler) Version 10.1.2.3.0 (Production)

Forms 10.1 (Form Compiler): Release  - Production

Copyright (c) 1982, 2005, Oracle.  All rights reserved.

PL/SQL Version 10.1.0.5.0 (Production)
Oracle Procedure Builder V10.1.2.3.0 - Production
Oracle Virtual Graphics System Version 10.1.2.0.0 (Production)
Oracle Multimedia Version 10.1.2.0.2 (Production)
Oracle Tools Integration Version 10.1.2.0.2 (Production)
Oracle Tools Common Area Version 10.1.2.0.2
Oracle CORE     10.1.0.5.0      Production
```

WHAT DEEP-DIVE SCRIPTS (continued)

WHAT SCHEMA STATS (S.BOMMAREDDY)

- What is the E-Business Suite Schema Statistics History (Execution Dates)?
- What is the E-Business Suite Schema Statistics History (Elapsed Time)?

Use this Script to quickly report on the E-Business Suite Gather Schema Statistics; the Statistics-History and Time-Consumed in generating the Statistics for each Schema.

Example:

```
#-----------------------------------------------------------------#
#- What Schema Statistics                       (whatschemastats) -#
#-----------------------------------------------------------------#

28-MAY-14        OATC (oratest) Apps Gather Schema Statistics
17:45:36         whatschemastats --  Gather Schema Statistics History

                 Schema             Schema             Elapsed Time
Scheam Name      Start Time         End-Time           Duration
---------------- ------------------ ------------------ ------------------
ABM              09-MAY-14 03:01:57 09-MAY-14 03:02:04 00:00:07
AHL              24-MAY-14 01:14:19 24-MAY-14 01:14:36 00:00:17
AHM              09-MAY-14 03:02:06 09-MAY-14 03:02:06 00:00:00
AK               24-MAY-14 01:14:36 24-MAY-14 01:15:01 00:00:25
ALR              24-MAY-14 01:15:01 24-MAY-14 01:15:14 00:00:13
AMF              09-MAY-14 03:02:25 09-MAY-14 03:02:25 00:00:00
AMS              24-MAY-14 01:15:14 24-MAY-14 01:15:52 00:00:38
AMV              24-MAY-14 01:15:52 24-MAY-14 01:16:01 00:00:09
AMW              24-MAY-14 01:16:01 24-MAY-14 01:16:16 00:00:15
AP               24-MAY-14 01:16:16 24-MAY-14 01:36:03 00:19:47
APPLSYS          24-MAY-14 01:36:03 24-MAY-14 01:44:24 00:08:21
APPS             24-MAY-14 01:44:24 24-MAY-14 01:47:23 00:02:59
AR               24-MAY-14 01:47:23 24-MAY-14 01:54:03 00:06:40
.
.
.
XLA              24-MAY-14 06:14:53 24-MAY-14 07:46:13 01:31:20
XLE              24-MAY-14 07:46:13 24-MAY-14 07:46:15 00:00:02
XNB              24-MAY-14 07:46:15 24-MAY-14 07:46:16 00:00:01
XNC              09-MAY-14 03:56:57 09-MAY-14 03:56:57 00:00:00
XNI              09-MAY-14 03:56:57 09-MAY-14 03:56:58 00:00:01
XNM              09-MAY-14 03:56:58 09-MAY-14 03:56:58 00:00:00
XNP              24-MAY-14 07:46:16 24-MAY-14 07:46:23 00:00:07
XNS              09-MAY-14 03:56:59 09-MAY-14 03:56:59 00:00:00
XTR              24-MAY-14 07:46:23 24-MAY-14 07:46:48 00:00:25
XXEIS            31-JAN-14 03:06:41 31-JAN-14 03:08:22 00:01:41
ZFA              24-MAY-14 07:46:48 24-MAY-14 07:46:48 00:00:00
ZPB              24-MAY-14 07:46:48 24-MAY-14 07:46:57 00:00:09
ZSA              24-MAY-14 07:46:57 24-MAY-14 07:46:57 00:00:00
ZX               24-MAY-14 07:46:57 24-MAY-14 07:53:59 00:07:02
```

WHAT DEEP-DIVE SCRIPTS (continued)

WHAT SCHEMA STATS DETAIL (M.BARONE)

- What is the E-Business Suite Schema Statistics Detail (Execution Dates)?
- What is the E-Business Suite Schema Statistics Detail History (Elapsed Time)?

Use this Script to quickly report on the E-Business Suite Gather Schema Statistics; the Statistics-History and Time-Consumed in generating the Statistics for each Object in each Schema and the Gather Schema Statistics Percent used.

Example:

```
#--------------------------------------------------------------#
#- What Schema Statistics Detail            (whatschemastats) -#
#--------------------------------------------------------------#

28-MAY-14       OATC (oratest) Apps Gather Schema Statistics
17:45:36        whatschemastats_detail --  Gather Schema Statistics History

                                    Elapsed
Schema   chema      Schema      Time     Estimate Object
Name    StartTime  End-Time    Duration  Percent Name
------ ---------- ---------- -------- -------- ------------------------------
AR      28-MAY-14  28-MAY-14   00:00:02      100 RA_INTERFACE_LINES_ALL
        09:16:39   09:16:41

AR      28-MAY-14  28-MAY-14   00:00:00      100 RA_INTERFACE_SALESCREDITS_ALL
        09:16:41   09:16:41

AR      28-MAY-14  28-MAY-14   00:00:01      100 RA_INTERFACE_DISTRIBUTIONS_ALL
        09:16:41   09:16:42

GL      28-MAY-14  28-MAY-14   00:00:01      100 GL_PERIOD_STATUSES
        14:12:01   14:12:02

XLA     28-MAY-14  28-MAY-14   00:13:23       40 XLA_AE_LINES
        14:11:01   14:24:24
```

WHAT DEEP-DIVE SCRIPTS (continued)

WHAT PROFILE (M.Barone)

- What are the E-Business Suite Profile Options and Profile Values?
- What E-Business Suite Profile Options are set at the Site/Application/Responsibility/User Levels?

Use this Script to quickly report on the E-Business Suite Profile-Options and Values. Additionally, this Scripts shows the Profile-Name, Profile-Level (Site, Application, Responsibility or User), the Profile-Last-Update-Date and the Profile-Value.

Example:

```
#-----------------------------------------------------------------#
#- eBusiness Suite 12.1 (whatprofile)                            -#
#-----------------------------------------------------------------#

28-MAY-14                  OATC (oratest) Profile Values
18:07:59                whatprofile   --  Sorted by ProfileName

User                                                  Last
Profile          Profile    Profile                   Update    Profile
Name             Name       Level      Context        Date      Value
---------------  ---------- ---------- ----------     --------- ---------------
OS: Site Use     AS_SITE_US Site                      04-MAY-00 MARKET
                 E

Site Name        SITENAME   Site                      15-APR-14 OATC Oracle
                                                                12.1 CRP1
                                                                (Cloned From
                                                                PROD 20May2013)
```

Please Note: **whatprofile** can be used to keep a HISTORY of PROFILE values. Each time this script executes and the Script-Search-Criteria is "%" is used to create this report, a complete list of ALL E-Business Suite Profile Option Values is created in the /tmp Directory.

So, you can easily see if and when a Profile Option has been changed.

WHAT DEEP-DIVE SCRIPTS (continued)

WHAT PROFILE CHANGE (M.BARONE)

- What E-Business Suite Profiles/Profile-Values Changed Since DD-MON-YY?

whatprofilechange uses the Profile and Profile Value Last_Update_Date. So, if the Profile or the Profile Value is changed multiple times, only the latest Last_Update_Date can be shown.

Use this Script to quickly report on the E-Business Suite Profile-Values that have changed SINCE a specified date. Additionally, this Scripts shows the Profile-Name, Profile-Level (Site, Application, Responsibility or User), the Profile-Last-Update-Date, the Profile-Value-Update-Date and the Profile-Value.

You can execute **whatprofilechange** daily if you are concerned that the E-Business Suite Profiles or Profile Values are changing and impacting your E-Business Suite environment.

Example:

```
19-JUN-14        OATC (oratest) Profile Values Changed Since
12:00:37         whatprofilechange  --  Sorted by ProfileName

                                                  Profile   Value
User                                              Last      Last
Profile               Profile                     Update    Update    Profile
Name                  Level      Context          Date      Date      Value
--------------------- ---------- ---------- --------- --------- ----------
ICX: Limit connect    Site                  06-JUL-06 19-JUN-14 1000
ICX: Limit time       Site                  06-JUL-06 19-JUN-14 480
ICX:Session Timeout   Site                  08-FEB-08 19-JUN-14 480
ICX:Session Timeout   User       BDUNHAM    08-FEB-08 19-JUN-14 480
ICX:Session Timeout   User       MBARONE    08-FEB-08 19-JUN-14 480
```

Chapter 4 – "What Database Detail Scripts"

WHAT DATABASE DETAIL SCRIPTS – WHAT ARE THEY ALL ABOUT?

The "what database detail scripts" are a series of operating system level scripts that interrogate the Oracle E-Business Suiteinternal tables for information not easily obtained through other means. These scripts were created to provide information quickly, accurately, and in an easy to read format.

The "what database detail scripts" are designed to assist System Administrators, Database Administrators, or really any IS/IT personnel looking for specific information such as what-forms-are-performing-poorly, and what-user-FormsIPAddresses-Are-RunAWays etc.. There are a wide variety of scripts found within this book. Please review the table of contents and appendixes to find a "what" script that best meets your needs.

WHAT DATABASE DETAIL SCRIPTS (continued)

WHAT DB FILES (M.Barone)

- What Database Files (DBF) are included in the E-Business Suite Database?

Use this Script to quickly list the E-Business Suite Database-Files for each Tablespace and the Database-File Names and Database File Sizes. Additionally, this Script will also list those Database Files that are in AutoExtend-Mode and the Maximum AutoExtend File-Size.

Example:

```
12-MAY-14                        Tablespace AutoExtend DBA Report     Page:    1
14:00:16                           Oracle Tablespace/File Name

                                                                            Auto
                                                                          Extend
                                                          Tablespace        Size Auto
Tablespace           DBF FileName                         Size(Bytes)    (Bytes) Extd
-------------------- ---------------------------- ------------ ----------- ----
APPS_TS_ARCHIVE      /d100/OATC/archive.dbf         3670016000           0 NO
APPS_TS_INTERFACE    /d100/OATC/interface.dbf       6291456000           0 NO
APPS_TS_MEDIA        /d100/OATC/media.dbf          22548578304           0 NO
APPS_TS_NOLOGGING    /d100/OATC/nologging.dbf        524288000           0 NO
APPS_TS_QUEUES       /d100/OATC/aq.dbf              1153433600           0 NO
APPS_TS_SEED         /d100/OATC/reference.dbf       1048576000           0 NO
APPS_TS_SUMMARY      /d100/OATC/summary.dbf         2097152000           0 NO
APPS_TS_TOOLS        /d100/OATC/apps_tools.dbf       524288000           0 NO
APPS_TS_TX_DATA      /d100/OATC/transaction.dbf    33285996544           0 NO
APPS_TS_TX_IDX       /d100/OATC/trans_idx.dbf      33285996544           0 NO
APPS_UNDOTS1         /d130/OATC/undo1.dbf          13958643712           0 NO
CTXSYS               /d100/OATC/ctxsys.dbf           524288000           0 NO
DISCO                /d100/OATC/DISCO.dbf           1073741824           0 NO
SYSAUX               /d100/OATC/sysaux.dbf          5368709120  5368709120 YES
SYSTEM               /d100/OATC/system.dbf          2747342848  4294967296 YES
TOAD                 /d100/OATC/toad01.dbf           262144000           0 NO
```

WHAT DATABASE DETAIL SCRIPTS (continued)

WHAT TEMP FILES (M.Barone)

- What Database TEMP Files are included in the E-Business Suite Database?

Use this Script to quickly list the E-Business Suite Database TEMP-Files. Additionally, this Script will also list those Database TEMP-Files that are in AutoExtend-Mode and the Maximum AutoExtend File-Size.

Example:

```
12-MAY-14                    Tablespace TEMP DBA Report              Page:    1
14:06:42                     Oracle Tablespace/File Name
                                                                        Auto
                                                                      Extend
                                                        Tablespace      Size Auto
Tablespace        Temp FileName                         Size(Bytes)   (Bytes) Extend
----------------- ------------------------------ ------------ -------- ------
TEMP              /d150/oradata/OATC/temp1.dbf    18874368000        0 NO
TEMP              /d150/oradata/OATC/temp2.dbf        5242880        0 NO
```

To Increase the TEMP Tablespace:

```
alter database tempfile '/d150/oradata/temp2.dbf' resize 1000M;
```

WHAT DATABASE DETAIL SCRIPTS (continued)

WHAT TEMP FREESPACE (M.Barone)

- What Database TEMP Files are included in the E-Business Suite Database?

Use this Script to quickly list the E-Business Suite Database TEMP-Files. Additionally, this Script will also list those Database TEMP-Files that are in AutoExtend-Mode and the Maximum AutoExtend File-Size.

WHAT TEMP FREESPACE (M.Barone)

- What Database TEMP Files are included in the E-Business Suite Database?

```
#----------------------------------------------------------------#
#- Oracle Database TEMP Freespace          (whattempfreespace) -#
#----------------------------------------------------------------#

30-MAY-12           OATC (oraprod) E-Business Database Report
14:10:37            E-Business Database TEMP Freespace

                 Num  Free             Total              Used         Free  Pct
TableSpace      DBFs  Frag         Space(Kb)         Space(Kb)    Space(Kb) Used
------------- ---- ----- ---------------- ---------------- ------------ ----
TEMP               5     0        18,452,480        18,452,480            0  100
                ---- ----- ---------------- ---------------- ------------
                   5     0        18,452,480        18,452,480            0
```

To Increase the TEMP Tablespace:

```
alter database tempfile '/d150/oradata/temp2.dbf' resize 1000M;
```

WHAT DATABASE DETAIL SCRIPTS (continued)

WHAT TEMP USAGE (M.Barone)

- What Database TEMP space is USED in the E-Business Suite Database?

Use this Script to quickly list the E-Business Suite Database TEMP-Space Used. This Script shows the TEMP Tablespace Total, TEMP Tablespace Used the TEMP Tablesapce Used Percent.

```
#----------------------------------------------------------------#
#- What (whattempusage)                                         -#
#----------------------------------------------------------------#

23-OCT-13                   Tablespace TEMP DBA Report            Page:    1
11:43:10                    Oracle TEMP Tablespace Usage

                                                 Tablespace
Tablespace                 Tablespace  Tablespace       Used
Name                             Used       Total        Pct
-------------------- ----------- ----------- -----------
TEMP                            90496     4926720    1.836841
```

WHAT DATABASE DETAIL SCRIPTS (continued)

WHAT TEMP USAGE DETAIL (M.Barone)

- What Database TEMP space is USED (detail) in the E-Business Database?

Use this Script to list the details of the E-Business Suite Database TEMP-Tablespace Used. This Script shows the TEMP Tablespace Objects, Extents and Space-Used (Bytes). The TEMP-Teblespace us heavily used so this will be a very large report.

```
#---------------------------------------------------------------#
#- What (whattempusage_detail)                                 -#
#---------------------------------------------------------------#

23-OCT-13                  Tablespace TEMP DBA Report              Page:    1
12:24:06                Oracle TEMP Tablespace Usage Detail

 System                                  Tablespace                             Tablespace
     ID UserNam Object Name  Program Name         Contents    Extents Size(Byte)
------- ------- ------------ ------- ---------- ---------- ------- --------
   1141 APPS    HZ_CUST_SITE frmweb@ TEMP        TEMPORARY        1     5120
                _USES_ALL    oatcinc
                             (TNS V3)

SQL Statement
----------------------------------------------------------------------
SELECT 1 FROM DUAL   WHERE EXISTS  (SELECT PF.INSTALLMENT_ID FROM GMS_
PROJECT_FUNDINGS PF , GMS_INSTALLMENTS INS   WHERE PF.INSTALLMENT_ID =
  INS.INSTALLMENT_ID  AND INS.AWARD_ID =  :b1    )
```

WHAT DATABASE DETAIL SCRIPTS (continued)

WHAT SEGMENT (M.Barone)

- What Database Segment Space is used by the E-Business Suite Database Schema/Segment -- Summary?

Use this Script to list the details of the E-Business Suite Database Objects/Segments stored in the E-Business Suite Database. This Script shows the Object-Owner, Tablespace-Name, Segment/Storage-Name, Segment-Type and Segment/Storage-Bytes-Used.

Example:

```
28-MAY-14              Oracle SegmentSpace Used by SchemaName          Page:    1
17:36:09              whatsegment -- Sorted by Tablespace Name

OWNER TABLESPACE_NAME SEGMENT_NAME                  SEGMENT_TYP           BYTES
----- --------------- ----------------------------- ----------- -------------
XDO   APPS_TS_TX_DATA SYS_IL0004319246C00010$$      LOBINDEX        2,621,440
XDO                   SYS_LOB0004319246C00010$$     LOBSEGMENT  1,421,213,696
XDO                   XDO_CONFIG_KEYS               TABLE             131,072
XDO                   XDO_CONFIG_PROPERTIES_B       TABLE             131,072
XDO                   XDO_CONFIG_PROPERTIES_TL      TABLE             131,072
XDO                   XDO_CONFIG_VALUES             TABLE             131,072
.
.
.
XDO                   XDO_FONT_MAPPING_SETS_TL      TABLE             131,072
XDO                   XDO_LOBS                      TABLE           3,670,016
XDO                   XDO_TEMPLATES_B               TABLE             524,288
XDO                   XDO_TEMPLATES_TL              TABLE             524,288
XDO                   XDO_TEMPLATE_FIELDS           TABLE           1,441,792
XDO                   XDO_TRANS_UNITS               TABLE           9,175,040
XDO                   XDO_TRANS_UNIT_PROPS          TABLE           1,048,576
XDO                   XDO_TRANS_UNIT_VALUES         TABLE           8,519,680
      ***************                                           -------------
      Total                                                     1,450,835,968

XDO   APPS_TS_TX_IDX  XDO_DS_DEFINITIONS_B_U1       INDEX             262,144
XDO                   XDO_DS_DEFINITIONS_TL_U1      INDEX             262,144
XDO                   XDO_DS_DEFINITIONS_TL_U2      INDEX             393,216
XDO                   XDO_LOBS_U1                   INDEX             786,432
.
.
.
XDO                   XDO_TRANS_UNITS_U1            INDEX           5,636,096
XDO                   XDO_TRANS_UNIT_PROPS_U1       INDEX             393,216
XDO                   XDO_TRANS_UNIT_VALUES_U1      INDEX           6,946,816
      ***************                                           -------------
      Total                                                        17,432,576
                                                                -------------
                                                                1,468,268,544
```

WHAT DATABASE DETAIL SCRIPTS (continued)

WHAT SEGMENT SPACE (M.Barone)

- What Database Segment Space is used by the E-Business Suite Database Tables/Indexes -- Detail ?

Use this Script to list the details of a specified/specific E-Business Suite Database Object(s)/Segment(s) stored in the E-Business Suite Database. This Script shows the Object-Owner, Tablespace-Name, Segment/Storage-Name, Segment-Type and Segment/Storage-Bytes-Used.

This Script is very useful for monitoring the TABLE or INDEX growth during an E-Business Suite Concurrent-Request or SQL-Operation.

Example:

```
21-MAY-14         Oracle SegmentSpace Used by SchemaName           Page:    1
17:46:37         whatsegment_space -- Sorted by Tablespace

Segment
           Tablesp                                  Segment              Space
Owner      Name    Segment Name                     Type                 Bytes
---------- ------- -------------------------------- ------- ----------------
XXOATC     OATCX   PA_IND_SETS_N6                   INDEX     4,866,990,080
           *******                                          ----------------
           Total                                              4,866,990,080
                                                            ----------------
                                                              4,866,990,080
```

WHAT DATABASE DETAIL SCRIPTS (continued)

WHAT INVALID (M.BARONE)

- What E-Business Suite Database Objects are INVALID -- Summary?

Use this Script to quickly summarize which E-Business Suite Database Objects (Functions, Packages, Package-Bodies, Procedures, Synonyms, Triggers and Views) are INVALID.

Example:

```
#---------------------------------------------------------------#
#- What (whatinvalid)                                          -#
#---------------------------------------------------------------#

                 OATC (oratest) Apps Invalid Objects          Page:    1
                 whatinvalid -- Sorted by Schema Name

Owner
Schema     Object Type               Count
---------- -------------------- ----------
APPS       FUNCTION                      2
           PACKAGE                       6
           PACKAGE BODY                  6
           PROCEDURE                     5
           SYNONYM                       1
           TRIGGER                       3
           VIEW                          2
**********                      ----------
Total                                   25
```

WHAT DATABASE DETAIL SCRIPTS (continued)

WHAT INVALID DETAIL (M.BARONE)

- What E-Business Suite Database Objects are INVALID -- Details?

Use this Script to quickly list the details about which E-Business Suite Database Objects (Functions, Packages, Package-Bodies, Procedures, Synonyms, Triggers and Views) are INVALID.

Example:

```
#-----------------------------------------------------------------#
#- What (whatinvaliddetail)                                      -#
#-----------------------------------------------------------------#

                 OATC (oratest) Apps Invalid Objects         Page:    1
               whatinvaliddetail -- Sorted by Schema Name

Owner
Schema     Object Name                              Object Type
---------- ---------------------------------------- --------------------
APPS       AHL_UTIL_UC_PKG                          PACKAGE BODY
           AP_CCE_BANK_UPGRADE                      PACKAGE BODY
           AP_PAYMENT_EVENT_WF_PKG                  PACKAGE BODY
           AR_CREDIT_CHECK                          PACKAGE
           AR_CREDIT_CHECK                          PACKAGE BODY
           AR_CREDIT_USAGE_RULE_SETS_VL             VIEW
           AR_INVOICE_API_PUB                       PACKAGE BODY
           ASO_CC_ENCRYPT_CONC_REQ_PVT              PACKAGE BODY
           AW_OAE3                                  PACKAGE
           AW_OAE3                                  PACKAGE BODY
           AW_USER_PROC                             PROCEDURE
           CSE_PROJ_TRANSFER_PKG                    PACKAGE BODY
           CSL_MTL_SYSTEM_ITEMS_ACC_PKG             PACKAGE BODY
           CS_ROUTING_UTL                           PACKAGE BODY

SYS        Q$LATCH                                  VIEW
           Q$LATCHSUM                               VIEW
```

WHAT DATABASE DETAIL SCRIPTS (continued)

WHAT DB LINKS (M.BARONE)

- What E-Business Suite Database Links ?

Use this Script to quickly list the details about which E-Business Suite Database Links and the Connection-String used to establish SQL-Connection.

Example:

```
#----------------------------------------------------------------#
#- What (whatdblink)                                             -#
#----------------------------------------------------------------#

28-NOV-14      oatcinc (oatcinc1.oatcinc.com) Apps Database Links
12:56:26                eBusiness DBA Database Links

                                                      Database Link
DBLink Owner    Database Link       DBLink User        HostName/Alias
--------------- ------------------ ------------------ ------------------
APPS            APPS_TO_APPS        APPS               ORAPROD
APPS            EDW_APPS_TO_WH      APPS               ORAPROD
```

WHAT DATABASE DETAIL SCRIPTS (continued)

WHAT INVALID RECOMPILE (M.Barone) (DBTier: executes using -- sqlplus / as sysdba)

- What E-Business Suite Database Objects are INVALID?
- This Script also ReCompiles ALL Invalid Objects and produces a Summary-List of the resulting INVALID Objects.

Use this Script to quickly RECOMPILE the E-Business Suite Database Objects (Functions, Packages, Package-Bodies, Procedures, Synonyms, Triggers and Views) that are INVALID.

Example:

```
#-----------------------------------------------------------------#
#- What (whatinvalidrecompile)                                   -#
#-----------------------------------------------------------------#

                  OATC (oratest) Apps Invalid Objects          Page:    1
                  whatrecompile -- Sorted by Schema Name

Owner!Sche Object Type                Count
---------- -------------------- ----------
APPS       FUNCTION                      2
           PACKAGE                       6
           PACKAGE BODY                  6
           PROCEDURE                     5
           SYNONYM                       1
           TRIGGER                       3
           VIEW                          2
**********                      ----------
Total                                   25
```

WHAT DATABASE DETAIL SCRIPTS (continued)

WHAT REGISTRY HISTORY (Roman Kab) (DBTier: executes using -- sqlplus / as sysdba)

What is the E-Business Database Registry History, Installation/Update/CPU/PSU?

Patch Set Updates (PSUs) are proactive cumulative patches containing recommended bug fixes that are released on a regular and predictable schedule. PSUs are on the same quarterly schedule as the Critical Patch Updates (CPU), specifically the Tuesday closest to the 17th of January, April, July, and October.

Critical Patch Updates are collections of security fixes for Oracle products. They are available to customers with valid support contracts. They are released on the Tuesday closest to the 17th day of January, April, July and October.

Example:

```
#----------------------------------------------------------------#
#- What (whatregistryhistory)                                   -#
#----------------------------------------------------------------#

06-JUN-14           OATC (oratest) Oracle Registry History
11:24:59    whatregistryhistory  --  EBusiness Oracle Database History

Action                                                           Bundle
Time      Version    Action  Name Space   ID Comments           Series
--------- ---------- ------- ---------- ---- ----------------- ----------
25-DEC-12 11.2.0.3.0 UPGRADE SERVER          Upgraded from
02.01.20                                     11.1.0.7.0

26-DEC-12 11.2.0.3   APPLY   SERVER      0   Patchset           PSU
05.06.17                                     11.2.0.2.0

26-DEC-12 11.2.0.3   APPLY   SERVER      1   PSU 11.2.0.3.1     PSU
07.23.13
```

WHAT DATABASE DETAIL SCRIPTS (continued)

WHAT DB VERSION (Tom Blanford) (DBTier: EXECUTES USING -- SQLPLUS / AS SYSDBA)

What is the E-Business Database Version ?
Is the Database in RESTRICTED mode (Permits ONLY SYS Privileged-User access.
Is the Database in ALLOWED mode (All Users can connect & access Database.

Example:

```
#-----------------------------------------------------------#
#- What Database Version  (RESTRICTED/LOGINS)              -#
#-----------------------------------------------------------#

06-JUN-14          OATC (oratest) Database Report
18:05:49           eBusiness Database Version Restrict/Logins

Database   Restricted
Version    Logins
---------- ----------
11.2.0.3.0 ALLOWED
```

WHAT DATABASE DETAIL SCRIPTS (continued)

WHAT DB FILES (MICHAEL BARONE) (DBTIER: EXECUTES USING -- SQLPLUS / AS SYSDBA)

What are the Database Files (DBFs) and where are they located ?
List ALL of the Database Files (DBFs) and Size, AutoExtend-Max-Size ?

Example:

```
2-OCT-15                     Tablespace AutoExtend DBA Report                    Page:    1
22:39:52                       Oracle Tablespace/File Name

                                                                                     Auto
                                                                                   Extend
                                                                         Tablespace    Size Auto
Tablespace          DBF FileName                                         Size(Bytes)  (Bytes) Extd
------------------- -------------------------------------------- ----------- ----------- ----
APPS_TS_ARCHIVE     /oracle/PROD/proddata/a_archive01.dbf            1097859072  2097152000 YES
APPS_TS_INTERFACE   /oracle/PROD/proddata/a_int01.dbf                1048576000  2097152000 YES
APPS_TS_MEDIA       /oracle/PROD/proddata/a_media01.dbf              2097152000  2097152000 YES
APPS_TS_MEDIA       /oracle/PROD/proddata/a_media02.dbf              2097152000  2097152000 YES
APPS_TS_MEDIA       /oracle/PROD/proddata/a_media03.dbf              2097152000  2097152000 YES
APPS_TS_MEDIA       /oracle/PROD/proddata/a_media04.dbf              2097152000  2097152000 YES
APPS_TS_MEDIA       /oracle/PROD/proddata/a_media05.dbf              2097152000  2097152000 YES
APPS_TS_MEDIA       /oracle/PROD/proddata/a_media06.dbf              2147483648  2147483648 YES
APPS_TS_MEDIA       /oracle/PROD/proddata/a_media07.dbf              2147483648  2147483648 YES
APPS_TS_MEDIA       /oracle/PROD/proddata/a_media08.dbf              2147483648           0 NO
APPS_TS_MEDIA       /oracle/PROD/proddata/a_media09.dbf              2147483648           0 NO
APPS_TS_MEDIA       /oracle/PROD/proddata/a_media10.dbf              2147483648           0 NO
APPS_TS_NOLOGGING   /oracle/PROD/proddata/a_nolog01.dbf               232914944  2097152000 YES
APPS_TS_QUEUES      /oracle/PROD/proddata/a_queue01.dbf               209715200  2097152000 YES
APPS_TS_SEED        /oracle/PROD/proddata/a_seed01.dbf               1048576000  2097152000 YES
APPS_TS_SEED        /oracle/PROD/proddata/a_seed02.dbf               1048576000  2097152000 YES
APPS_TS_SUMMARY     /oracle/PROD/proddata/a_summ01.dbf               1048576000  2097152000 YES
APPS_TS_TOOLS       /oracle/PROD/proddata/a_tools01.dbf               104857600           0 NO
APPS_TS_TX_DATA     /oracle/PROD/proddata/a_txn_data01.dbf           2097152000           0 NO
APPS_TS_TX_DATA     /oracle/PROD/proddata/a_txn_data02.dbf           2097152000           0 NO
APPS_TS_TX_IDX      /oracle/PROD/proddata/a_txn_ind01.dbf            2097152000           0 NO
APPS_TS_TX_IDX      /oracle/PROD/proddata/a_txn_ind02.dbf            2097152000           0 NO
APPS_UNDOTS1        /oracle/PROD/proddata/undo01.dbf                 1520435200  2097152000 YES
APPS_UNDOTS1        /oracle/PROD/proddata/undo02.dbf                 1509949440  2097152000 YES
APPS_UNDOTS1        /oracle/PROD/proddata/undo03.dbf                 1520435200  2097152000 YES
CTXD                /oracle/PROD/proddata/ctxd01.dbf                  104857600           0 NO
EUL                 /oracle/PROD/proddata/euld01.dbf                  161480704  2097152000 YES
INTERIM             /oracle/PROD/proddata/interim.dbf                 209715200           0 NO
NOETIXD             /oracle/PROD/proddata/noetix01.dbf                681639936  1572864000 YES
OWAPUB              /oracle/PROD/proddata/owad01.dbf                   10485760  1048576000 YES
PORTAL              /oracle/PROD/proddata/portal01.dbf                314572800           0 NO
SYSAUX              /oracle/PROD/proddata/sysaux01.dbf               1825112064 ########### YES
SYSTEM              /oracle/PROD/proddata/system01.dbf               1572864000           0 NO
SYSTEM              /oracle/PROD/proddata/system02.dbf               1572864000           0 NO
SYSTEM              /oracle/PROD/proddata/system03.dbf               2097152000           0 NO
SYSTEM              /oracle/PROD/proddata/system04.dbf               1572864000           0 NO
SYSTEM              /oracle/PROD/proddata/system05.dbf               1572864000           0 NO
SYSTEM              /oracle/PROD/proddata/system06.dbf               1572864000           0 NO
SYSTEM              /oracle/PROD/proddata/system07.dbf               1572864000           0 NO
XXEISD              /oracle/PROD/proddata/xxeis_tab.dbf               524288000 ########### YES
XXEISX              /oracle/PROD/proddata/xxeis_ind.dbf               524288000 ########### YES
```

WHAT DATABASE DETAIL SCRIPTS (continued)

WHAT SYSSTAT PARALLEL (MIKE SWING) (DBTIER: EXECUTES USING -- SQLPLUS / AS SYSDBA)

What is the E-Business Database Database Parallel-Execution-Results ?

PARALLEL_MAX_SERVERS is the Maximum Number of Parallel-Execution-Server-Processes. Once the PARALLEL_MAX_SERVERS value is reached, no new PARALLEL servers processes are started. When a SQL-Statement is launched with DEGREE OF PARALLELISM, the Query-Coordinator recruits the requested-number of PARALLEL-EXECUTION-SERVERS.

When the SQL-Statement's DEGREE OF PARALLELISM is larger-than PARALLEL_MAX_SERVERS or larger-than the available PARALLEL-SERVERS, the SQL-Statement will execute in reduced PARALLELISM or in SERIAL.

PARALLEL_MIN_SERVERS is the Minimum Number of Parallel-Execution-Server-Processes. (DEFAULT=0). When you specify PARALLEL_MIN_SERVERS > 0 Oracle will hold ALL SQL-Statements until the MINIMUM-PARALLEL-EXECUTION-SERVERS are available.

Example:

```
#-----------------------------------------------------------------#
#- What (whatsysstat_parallel)                                   -#
#-----------------------------------------------------------------#

14-AUG-12      [(ORAPROD) V$SYSSTAT Parallel-Execution Results]
15:03:09

                                                         VSYSSTAT
VSYSSTAT Table Name                                                 Value
------------------------------------------------------------ --------
Parallel operations downgraded 1 to 25 pct                              0
Parallel operations downgraded 25 to 50 pct                           190
Parallel operations downgraded 50 to 75 pct                            25
Parallel operations downgraded 75 to 99 pct                             0
Parallel operations downgraded to serial                               60
Parallel operations not downgraded                                   1536

Please see /tmp/whatsysstat_parallel_9010.txt
```

CHAPTER 5 – "WHAT PERFORMANCE SCRIPTS"

WHAT PERFORMANCE SCRIPTS – WHAT ARE THEY ALL ABOUT?

The "what performance scripts" are a series of operating system level scripts that interrogate the Oracle E-Business Suiteinternal tables for information not easily obtained through other means. These scripts were created to provide information quickly, accurately, and in an easy to read format.

The "what performance scripts" are designed to assist System Administrators, Database Administrators, or really any IS/IT personnel looking for specific information such as what-forms-are-performing-poorly, and what-user-FormsIPAddresses-Are-RunAWays etc.. There are a wide variety of scripts found within this book. Please review the table of contents and appendixes to find a "what" script that best meets your needs.

WHAT PERFORMANCE SCRIPTS (continued)

WHAT CONC MGR SESSIONS (MATT MULLIN)

- What Concurrent Manager Database Sessions are ACTIVE/RUNNING?

Use this Script to quickly list the details about the E-Business Suite Concurrent-Manager Sessions. This Script shows the Concurrent-Program-Session, the Concurrent-Manager-Connect-Date, the AppsTier-Unix-Process-ID, the DBTier-Unix-Process-ID, the Oracle-Database_SID and Oracle-Database-Serial#, and the Concurrent-Manager-Last-Call-Date.

Example:

```
28-MAY-14                 oratest OATC DBA Report                  Page:    1
16:23-51    whatconcmgrsessions Oracle Sessions Assigned to ConcMgrs

                                              AppsTier DBTier
ConcMgr        ConcMgr                        Unix     UNIX     Oracle Oracle
Program        Program         Connect        Process  Process  System Serial Last
Session        Process         Date           ID       ID          SID Number Call
-------------- ------------ ------- -------- -------- ------ ------ -------
ICM@oratst     oracle@orats 25MAY13 20054076 23986406   1006     83 28MAY13
FNDSM@oratst   oracle@orats 25MAY13 19398862 14418276   1754     17 28MAY13
PODAMGR@orats  oracle@orats 25MAY13 5177384  19988910      8     15 28MAY13
JDBC ThinClie  oracle@orats 25MAY13 34406604 7536922    1541     13 28MAY13
FNDLIBR@orats  oracle@orats 25MAY13 23331016 53477598   1788     17 28MAY13
FNDLIBR@orats  oracle@orats 25MAY13 29032626 13959502     38     13 28MAY13

STANDARD@orat  oracle@orats 25MAY13 20316236 12320934   1796    497 28MAY13
STANDARD@orat  oracle@orats 25MAY13 5243124  63439000    505   5597 28MAY13
STANDARD@orat  oracle@orats 25MAY13 15597686 28115062   1559  23313 28MAY13
STANDARD@orat  oracle@orats 25MAY13 12451866 34537692     51  11369 28MAY13
STANDARD@orat  oracle@orats 25MAY13 9765092  58392786   1077   1435 28MAY13
```

WHAT PERFORMANCE SCRIPTS (continued)

WHAT SESSION (M.BARONE) (DBTIER: EXECUTES USING -- SQLPLUS / AS SYSDBA)

- What E-Business Suite Database Sessions are ACTIVE/INACTIVE?
- What Program are these Sessions Executing?
- What Database Background Sessions (PMON, SMON, LGWR, DIAG are ACTIVE?

Use this **whatsession** to quickly list the details about the E-Business Suite Datbase Sessions. **whatsession** shows the OS-User, the User-Name, the DBTier-Unix-Process-ID, the Database-Program-Name and the Status (Active/Inactive).

Example:

```
28-MAY-14                    oratest OATC DBA Report                  Page:    1
16:23-51                whatsession  --  Oracle Current Session(s)

                           UNIX      Oracle Oracle
         User     Process   System Serial
OS User  Name     ID           SID Number Program                  Status
-------- -------- -------- ------ ------ ------------------------ --------
applmgr  APPS     30802110      9     11 PODAMGR@oatcapd04  (TNS  ACTIVE
applmgr  APPS     56557806     47     31 JDBC Thin Client         ACTIVE
applmgr  APPS     13042002   1860  16041 frmweb@oatcapd04  (TNS   INACTIVE
wddunha  RFREADON 43319404    811   2511 Toad.exe                 INACTIVE
oracle            37617776      1      1 oracle@oatcdbd03  (DIA0) ACTIVE
oracle            7143576       2      1 oracle@oatcdbd03  (LGWR) ACTIVE
oracle            47972450      3     11 oracle@oatcdbd03  (QMNC) ACTIVE
oracle            52560102      5      1 oracle@oatcdbd03  (Q003) ACTIVE
oracle            35127540    251      1 oracle@oatcdbd03  (MMAN) ACTIVE
oracle            7930134     252      1 oracle@oatcdbd03  (CKPT) ACTIVE
oracle            44302440    253      5 oracle@oatcdbd03  (CJQ0) ACTIVE
oracle            17498174    501      1 oracle@oatcdbd03  (PMON) ACTIVE
oracle            33292494    502      1 oracle@oatcdbd03  (DBW0) ACTIVE
oracle            20906014    503      1 oracle@oatcdbd03  (SMON) ACTIVE
oracle            47448084    751      1 oracle@oatcdbd03  (PSP0) ACTIVE
oracle            22347894    752      1 oracle@oatcdbd03  (DBW1) ACTIVE
oracle            45613172    753      1 oracle@oatcdbd03  (RECO) ACTIVE
oracle            25165992    848   5617 oracle@oatcdbd03  (W006) ACTIVE
oracle            53280808   1001      1 oracle@oatcdbd03  (VKTM) ACTIVE
oracle            19660874   1002      1 oracle@oatcdbd03  (DBW2) ACTIVE
oracle            47054928   1003      1 oracle@oatcdbd03  (MMON) ACTIVE
oracle            50987206   1056   2411 oracle@oatcdbd03  (J000) ACTIVE
oracle            41812024   1251      1 oracle@oatcdbd03  (GEN0) ACTIVE
oracle            16777320   1252      1 oracle@oatcdbd03  (DBW3) ACTIVE
oracle            51445764   1253      1 oracle@oatcdbd03  (MMNL) ACTIVE
oracle            48562184   1255      1 oracle@oatcdbd03  (Q000) ACTIVE
oracle            54001878   1338  21091 oracle@oatcdbd03  (J001) ACTIVE
oracle            38797368   1501      1 oracle@oatcdbd03  (DIAG) ACTIVE
oracle            16187630   1502      1 oracle@oatcdbd03  (DBW4) ACTIVE
oracle            38666334   1506      5 oracle@oatcdbd03  (SMCO) ACTIVE
oracle            48037902   1752      1 oracle@oatcdbd03  (DBRM) ACTIVE
oracle            10027188   1753      1 oracle@oatcdbd03  (DBW5) ACTIVE
oracle            42270778   1757      3 oracle@oatcdbd03  (M001) ACTIVE
oracle            39190606   1850   1415 oracle@oatcdbd03  (W002) ACTIVE

412 rows selected
```

WHAT PERFORMANCE SCRIPTS (continued)

WHAT SESSION BACKGROUND (MATT MULLIN)

- What Database Sessions are assigned to Datatbase Background tasks?

Use **whatsessionbackground** to quickly list the details about the E-Business Suite Database Background Sessions. **whatsessionbackground** shows the Database-Background-Session, the Database-Background-Connect-Date, the AppsTier-Unix-Process-ID, the DBTier-Unix-Process-ID, the Oracle-Database_SID and Oracle-Database-Serial#, and the Database-Background-Last-Call-Date.

Example:

```
01-MAY-14                    oratest OATC DBA Report                 Page:    1
08:35-32           whatsessbackground Oracle Sessions Assigned to
                             Database Background Processes

                                                AppsTier DBTier
Background Background                           Unix     UNIX    Oracle Oracle
Program    Program      Connect                 Process  Process System Serial
Session    Process      Date                    ID       ID         SID Number Last Call
---------- -----------  ---------               -------- ------- ------ ------ ---------
oracle@ora oracle@orat  30-JUN-14               2294154  2294154    501      1 30-JUN-14
test(PMON) test (PMON)

oracle@ora oracle@orat  30-JUN-14               5898730  5898730   1501      1 30-JUN-14
(DIAG)     est (DIAG)

oracle@ora oracle@orat  30-JUN-14               53346452 53346452  1752      1 30-JUN-14
(DBRM)     est (DBRM)

oracle@ora oracle@orat  30-JUN-14               61210836 61210836   251      1 30-JUN-14
(MMAN)     est (MMAN)

oracle@ora oracle@orat  30-JUN-14               26018034 26018034   502      1 30-JUN-14
(DBW0)     est (DBW0)

oracle@ora oracle@orat  30-JUN-14               11665530 11665530     2      1 30-JUN-14
(LGWR)     est (LGWR)

oracle@ora oracle@orat  30-JUN-14               19922944 19922944   252      1 30-JUN-14
(CKPT)     est (CKPT)

oracle@ora oracle@orat  30-JUN-14               40370402 40370402   503      1 30-JUN-14
(SMON)     est (SMON)

oracle@ora oracle@orat  30-JUN-14               55509164 55509164   753      1 30-JUN-14
(RECO)     est (RECO)

oracle@ora oracle@orat  30-JUN-14               23986416 23986416  1003      1 30-JUN-14
(MMON)     est (MMON)

. . .
oracle@ora oracle@orat  01-JUL-14               39452770 39452770  1032   5177 01-JUL-14
(W000)     est (W000)
```

WHAT PERFORMANCE SCRIPTS (continued)

WHAT SESSION CONCURRENT REQUEST (MATT MULLIN)

- What Database Sessions are assigned to Datatbase Concurrent Requests?

Use **whatsessconcreq** to quickly list the details about the E-Business Suite Database Concurrent-Request Sessions. **whatsessconcreq** shows the Database-Concurrent-Request-Sessions, the Database-Concurrent-Request-Connect-Date, the AppsTier-Unix-Process-ID, the DBTier-Unix-Process-ID, the Oracle-Database_SID and Oracle-Database-Serial#, and the Database-Concurrent-Request-Last-Call-Date.

Example:

```
01-MAY-13              srfodbt03 RFTESTX DBA Report                  Page:    1
18:25-59         Oracle Session(s) -- Assigned to ConcMgrs
                             whatsessconcreq

                                          AppsTier DBTier
ConcMgr      ConcMgr                      Unix     UNIX     Oracle Oracle
Program      Program      Connect         Process  Process  System Serial
Session      Process      Date            ID       ID          SID Number Last Call
------------ ------------ --------- -------- -------- ------ ------ ---------
STANDARD@oat oracle@oatc  01-MAY-14 39845988 14680074   1010    739 01-MAY-14
c(TNS V1-V3)

PYUGEN@oatc  oracle@oatc  19-NOV-13 29753508 43581512   2147     35 01-MAY-14
(TNS V1-V3)

PYUGEN@oatc  oracle@oatc  19-NOV-13 29753510 43581514   2149     37 01-MAY-14
(TNS V1-V3)

PYUGEN@oatc  oracle@oatc  19-NOV-13 29753512 43581516   2151     39 01-MAY-14
(TNS V1-V3)

PYUGEN@oatc  oracle@oatc  19-NOV-13 29753514 43581518   2153     41 01-MAY-14
(TNS V1-V3)
```

WHAT PERFORMANCE SCRIPTS (continued)

WHAT SESSION CONCURRENT REQUEST IO (MATT MULLIN)

- What Database Sessions are assigned to Datatbase Concurrent Requests?

Use **whatsessconcreq_io** to quickly list the details about the E-Business Suite Database Concurrent Request Session I/O activity. **Whatsessconcreq_io** shows the Database-Concurrent-Request-Session, the Database-Concurrent-Request AppsTier-Unix-Process-ID, the DBTier-Unix-Process-ID, the Oracle-Database Physical Reads (Read from Disk), Block Gets (Block Reads from Disk), Consisten-Gets (Reads from Memory), Block Changes (Updates/Writes) and Consistent Changes Updates/Changes to data in Memory).

Example:

```
01-MAY-14                 oratest OATC DBA Report           Page:    1
18:25-37              Oracle Session(s) -- Assigned to ConcMgrs
                                     whatsessconcreq_io
```

ConcMgr Program Session	AppsTier Unix Process ID	DBTier UNIX Process ID	DB-IO Physical Reads	DB-IO Block Gets	DB-IO Consist Gets	DB-IO Block Changes	DB-IO Consist Changes
STANDARD@oatc (TNS V1-V3)	39845988	14680074	186138	67	262473	79	30
PYUGEN@oatc (TNS V1-V3)	29753508	43581512	11442210	1650	112010	110	130
PYUGEN@oatc (TNS V1-V3)	29753510	43581512	14422410	1670	114410	120	140
PYUGEN@oatc (TNS V1-V3)	29753512	43581512	14426010	1690	114510	210	160
PYUGEN@oatc (TNS V1-V3)	29753514	43581512	14428010	1710	114710	212	190

WHAT PERFORMANCE SCRIPTS (continued)

WHAT JVM/JDBC SESSION (M.BARONE)

- What Unix/Linux Sessions are assigned to JVM/JDBC Connections ?

Use **whatjvmsession** to quickly list the details about the E-Business Suite Database Sessions used by JVM/JDBC Connections. **Whatsjvmsession** shows the Mchine/Server Initiating the Connection, the AppsTier-Unix-Process-ID, the AppsTier Program Name, the AppsTier JVM/JDBC Module, and the summary count of JVM/JDBC Connections.

Example:

```
01-MAY-14                  oratest OATC DBA Report                 Page:    1
18:25-37              Oracle Current JVM/JDBC Session(s)
                                whatjvmsession

             Unix
Machine      Process JVM/JDBC Program      JVM/JDBC Module             Count
------------ ------- --------------------- ------------------------ --------
rduora-prod  30459   JDBC Thin Client      JDBC Thin Client                4
rduora-prod          JDBC Thin Client      fnd.wf.worklist.server.D        1
                                           ummyAM:R

rduora-prod          JDBC Thin Client      fnd.framework.server.OAA        2
                                           pplicationModule

rduora-prod          JDBC Thin Client      pos.changeorder.server.V        1
                                           iewOrderAM

rduora-prod          JDBC Thin Client      icx.por.rcv.server.Recei        1
                                           vingHomeAM:R
rduora-prod          JDBC Thin Client      fnd.framework.navigate.s        1
                                           erver.OANavigatePortletA

rduora-prod          JDBC Thin Client      icx.por.rcv.server.Recei        1
                                           veItemsAM

rduora-prod          JDBC Thin Client      fnd.wf.worklist.server.W        1
                                           orklistAM:R

rduora-prod          JDBC Thin Client      icx.por.common.server.La        1
                                           unchIPAM

rduora-prod          JDBC Thin Client      fnd.wf.worklist.server.N        1
                                           otificationsAM:R

rduora-prod          JDBC Thin Client      fnd.wf.worklist.server.W        1
                                           orklistAM

rduora-prod          JDBC Thin Client      icx.por.req.server.Requi        5
                                           sitionAM
```

WHAT PERFORMANCE SCRIPTS (continued)

WHOS UP_SESSIONS (M.BARONE)

- Who is Connected and What Database Sessions are assigned to those Oracle-Forms (**frmweb**) connections?

Use **whosupsessions** to quickly list the details about the E-Business Suite connected-Users.. **whosupsessions** shows the Program-Session, Connect-Date, AppsTier-Unix-Process-ID, DBTier-Unix-Process-ID, Database-SID, Database-Serial#, and the DB & Form Server AUDSID.

The AUDSID is the ID the ties the AppsTier-Sessions the the DBTier-Sessions.

When the Oracle E-Business Suite User launches an Oracle Form, there are two (2) Database Sessions that are created.

- The First Datbase Session (below) is the E-Business Connection (DB-Form Server AUDSID: 86492123)
- The Second Database Session (below) is the E-Business Suite Form (DB-Form Server AUDSID: 86492124)

Please Note that the matching **AppsTier UNIX Process ID** is displayed on both the **whosup** screen (above) and on the **whosup_sessions** and the **whosup_sessions_io** screens (below).

Example:

```
#-----------------------------------------------------------------#
#- Oracle Database Sessions Assigned to Forms Connections       -#
#-----------------------------------------------------------------#

09-JUL-12                  oratest OATC DBA Report                  Page:    1
19:51-11        Oracle Session(s) -- Assigned to frmweb-Connections

                                         AppsTier DBTier
                                         UNIX     UNIX      Oracle Oracle DB & Form
Program         Program    Connect       Process  Process   System Serial Server
Session         Process    Date          ID       ID           SID Number AUDSID
--------------- ---------- ---------- -------- --------- ------ ------ --------
frmweb@oratest  oracle@or  09-JUL-12  26149062 50266218    1523    415 86496123
(TNS V1-V3)     atest

frmweb@oratest  oracle@or  09-JUL-12  26149062 50266218    1531    223 86496124
(TNS V1-V3)     atest
```

WHAT PERFORMANCE SCRIPTS (continued)

WHOS UP_SESSIONS_IO (M.BARONE)

- Who is Connected and What Database Sessions I/O Activity is occurring on those Oracle-Forms (**frmweb**) Connections?

Use **whosupsessions_io** to quickly list the Input/Output details about the E-Business Suite connected-Users.. **whosupsessions_io** shows the Program-Session, AppsTier-Unix-Process-ID, DBTier-Unix-Process-ID, Database-Physical-Read, Database-Block-Gets, Database-Consistent (in-Memory) Gets, Database Block Changes and Database Consistent Changes.

```
09-JUL-12                     oratest OATC DBA Report                Page:    1
19:51-50         Oracle Session(s) -- Assigned to frmweb-Connections

            AppsTier DBTier
Forms       Unix     UNIX                DB-IO    DB-IO       DB-IO   DB-IO    DB-IO
Program     Process  Process          Physical    Block     Consist   Block  Consist
Session     ID       ID                  Reads     Gets        Gets  Changs   Changs
----------- -------- -------- ---------- -------- ---------- -------- -------
frmweb@orat 26149062 50266218         1679      186   10013647       83      24
(TNS V1-V3)

frmweb@orat 26149062 50266218        11804      164   32119315       65      90
(TNS V1-V3)
```

WHAT PERFORMANCE SCRIPTS (continued)
WHOS UP_SESSIONS (CONTINUED) (M.BARONE)

Please Note: The AppsTier Server's Unix-Processes can also be manually interrogated:

AppsTier/FormServerTier:
Use the Unix/Linux/AIX Command **ps -efa | grep frmweb**
to quickly list the AppsTier/FormServerTier to FormWeb Sessions.

The AppsTier/FormServer Tier FormWeb shows the **PC-Client IP-Address**

```
[UNIX/Linux/AIX]  ps -efa | grep frmweb
applmgr 26149062 214800 frmweb server webfile=HTTP-,0,1,default,10.20.100.127
```

Also Note: A Desktop PC can be used to determine the User's Neme from the IPAddress

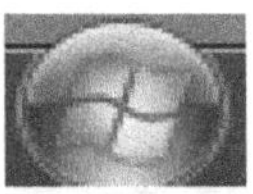
Start

Search Programs and Files

Type **CMD** **in the Search Programs and Files Box**

```
c:\>nslookup 10.20.100.127
Server:   oatc.oatcinc.com
Address:   10.10.10.10

Name:     oatc.oatcinc.com
Address:   10.20.100.127

Name:     mbarone.oatc.oatcinc.com
Address:   10.20.100.127
```

In the Command) Window, type. **nslookup XXX.XXX.XXX.XXX**

Where ###.###.###.### is the
IPAddress from the Unix/Linux Screen (above).

Example: **nslookup 10.20.100.127**

WHAT PERFORMANCE SCRIPTS (continued)

WHOSUP + WHOSUP_SESSIONS + WHOSUP_SESSION_IO (M.BARONE)

Use **whosup** and **whosup_sessions** and **whosup_session_io** to navigate all the way from the ClientPC to the AppsTier and all the way to the DatabaseTier

whosup

```
#-----------------------------------------------------------------#
#- ICX Connections (whosup)                                      -#
#-----------------------------------------------------------------#
10-SEP-13                      Apps ICX Connections
13:18:36                        Sorted by UserName
                                                                          Last
                                                                 ICX       ICX
UserName User Description    Responsibility                   Connect   Activity
-------- ------------------- -----------------------------    --------- --------
94813    Carpenter, Mr. Ken US Super HRMS Manager             10-SEP-13 10-SEP-13
                                                              11:01:52  11:06:59


#-----------------------------------------------------------------#
#- Forms Connections (whosup)                                    -#
#-----------------------------------------------------------------#
10-SEP-13                         Apps FormServer
13:18:37                        Sorted by UserName

                    Apps                           Apps     Apps          Form
                    Short                FormStart Server   Server      Server
User   FormName     Name  Responsibility Time      ProcID   Name        AUDSID
------ ------------ ----- -------------- --------- -------- ------- ---------
94813  Authenticat BEN    US Super HRMS  10-SEP-13 29229254 srfoapd  86766811
       the person          Manager        11:06:45           04
```

WHAT PERFORMANCE SCRIPTS (continued)
WHOSUP + WHOSUP_SESSIONS + WHOSUP_SESSION_IO (M.BARONE)

Use **whosup** and **whosup_sessions** and **whosup_session_io** to navigate all the way from the ClientPC to the AppsTier and all the way to the DatabaseTier

whosup_sessions

```
#-----------------------------------------------------------------#
#- Forms Connections Details (whosup_sessions)                    -#
#-----------------------------------------------------------------#
10-MAY-14                      OATC DBA Report                     Page:    1
13:17-29     Oracle Session(s) -- Assigned to frmweb-Connections
                               whosup_sessions

                                                AppsTier DBTier
Forms           Forms                           Unix     UNIX     Oracle Oracle DB-Form
Program         Program      Forms              Process  Process  System Serial Server
Session         Process      Date               ID       ID          SID Number AUDSID
--------------- ----------- --------- -------- -------- ----- ------ --------
frmweb@srfoapd oracle@srfo 10-SEP-13 29229254 45744536   197    233 86766811
04 (TNS V1-V3) dbd03
```

whosup_sessions_io

```
#-----------------------------------------------------------------#
#- Forms Connections I/O (whosup_sessions-io)                     -#
#-----------------------------------------------------------------#
10-MAY-14                      OATC DBA Report                     Page:    1
13:26-58    Oracle Session(s) -- Assigned to frmweb-Connections
                            whosup_sessions_io

          AppsTier DBTier
Forms     Unix     UNIX          DB-IO    DB-IO      DB-IO    DB-IO   DB-IO
Program   Process  Process    Physical    Block    Consist    Block Consist
Session   ID       ID            Reads     Gets       Gets  Changes Changes
---------- -------- -------- ---------- -------- ---------- -------- -------
frmweb@   29229254 45744536        303  5495494  441325861  4485481
oatc04
```

WHAT PERFORMANCE SCRIPTS (continued)

WHOSUP + WHOSUP_SESSIONS + WHOSUP_SESSION_IO (M.BARONE)

Use **whosup** and **whosup_sessions** and **whosup_session_io** to navigate all the way from the ClientPC to the AppsTier and all the way to the DatabaseTier

whosup_sessions_io

```
#----------------------------------------------------------------#
#- Forms Connections I/O (whosup_sessions-io)                   -#
#----------------------------------------------------------------#
10-MAY-14                          OATC, DBA Report                 Page:    1
13:26-58    Oracle Session(s) -- Assigned to frmweb-Connections
                                whosup_sessions_io

           AppsTier DBTier
Forms      Unix     UNIX          DB-IO    DB-IO      DB-IO    DB-IO   DB-IO
Program    Process  Process    Physical    Block    Consist    Block Consist
Session    ID       ID            Reads     Gets       Gets  Changes Changes
---------- -------- -------- ---------- -------- ---------- -------- -------
frmweb@    29229254 45744536        303  5495494  441325861  4485481
oatc04
```

30-Seconds Later

whosup_sessions_io

```
#----------------------------------------------------------------#
#- Forms Connections I/O (whosup_sessions-io) Showing Spinning -#
#- DB-IO-Physical-Read (Column) vs DB-IO-Consist-Gets (Column) -#
#- Shows NO Physical-Read, but IO-Gets increased by 11 Million -#
#----------------------------------------------------------------#
10-MAY-14                          OATC, DBA Report                 Page:    1
13:30-30    Oracle Session(s) -- Assigned to frmweb-Connections
                                whosup_sessions_io

           AppsTier DBTier
Forms      Unix     UNIX          DB-IO    DB-IO      DB-IO    DB-IO   DB-IO
Program    Process  Process    Physical    Block    Consist    Block Consist
Session    ID       ID            Reads     Gets       Gets  Changes Changes
---------- -------- -------- ---------- -------- ---------- -------- -------
frmweb@    29229254 45744536        305  5504070  452716937  4494828      13
oatc
```

WHAT PERFORMANCE SCRIPTS (continued)

WHATSQL F.BENDER)

Use **whatsql** to quickly list the ACTIVE and INACTIVE sql in the SQLText Area.

Session AUDSID maps the DBTier-Process with the AppsTier-Process.

Session AUDSID can be used in the E-BusinessSuite Oracle Application Manager to Turn-ON/OFF Database Trace and collect more information:
System Administrator <Responsibility>
Oracle Application Manager → Dashboard → Monitoring

Session AUDSID can be used in the E-Business Suite Oracle Applicatin Manager to Terminate the DBTier and AppsTier sessions and processes:
System Administrator <Responsibility>
Oracle Application Manager → Dashboard → Monitoring

Unix ID Can be used to Kill/Terminate the Unix/Linux process.

whatsql

```
#----------------------------------------------------------------#
#- What SQL is Executing                                        -#
#----------------------------------------------------------------#
10-MAY-14                [OATC (oraprod) Apps SQLText]
19:07:01

Unix    Oracle     Session Unix  Oracle Oracle Session
User    User        AUDSID ID     Sessn Serial Status    SQL Text
------- ------ ---------- ----- ------ ------ --------- ----------------------
oracle  APPS    428783483 69768   3401  36357 ACTIVE    SELECT S.ROWID ROW_ID
                                                        FROM
                                                        WF_ITEM_ACTIVITY_STATU
                                                        SES WHERE S.D
                                                        UE_DATE < SYSDATE AND
                                                        S.ACTIVITY_STATUS IN
                                                        ('ACTIVE','WAITING','
                                                        NOTIFIED',
                                                        'SUSPEND','DEFERRED')

#----------------------------------------------------------------#
#- What SQL is Executing                                        -#
#----------------------------------------------------------------#
10-MAY-14                [OATC (oraprod) Apps SQLText]
19:07:01

Unix    Oracle     Session Unix  Oracle Oracle Session
User    User        AUDSID ID     Sessn Serial Status    SQL Text
------- ------ ---------- ----- ------ ------ --------- ----------------------
oracle  APPS    428783483 69768   3401  36357 ACTIVE    SELECT S.ROWID ROW_ID
                                                        FROM
                                                        WF_ITEM_ACTIVITY_STATU
                                                        SES WHERE S.D
                                                        UE_DATE < SYSDATE AND
                                                        S.ACTIVITY_STATUS IN
                                                        ('ACTIVE','WAITING','
                                                        NOTIFIED',
                                                        'SUSPEND','DEFERRED')
```

WHAT PERFORMANCE SCRIPTS (continued)

WHATBLOCK (M.BARONE)

Use **whatblock** to quickly identify BLOCKING-LOCKS on Database-Objects. **Whatblock** shows the Database-Session that is holding the Lock and the Database-Session(s) that is trying to get a lock on the same Database-Object.

whatblock

```
#----------------------------------------------------------------#
#- whatblock -- What Objects are Locked                         -#
#----------------------------------------------------------------#
10-SEP-13             Oracle Blocking Locks By User Name              Page:    1
13:17:03         whatblock -- Sorted By Object and Locker-ID
C=Share/Row-Exclusive L=RowShare N=No-Lock R=RowExclusive S=Share X=Exclusive

      Object                Session Session Session                 Lock Rqst Lock
User  Name                  Sid     Serial  AudSid   Program        Mode Mode Type
----- ---------------- ------- ------- -------- -------------- ---- ---- ----
APPS  BEN_PERSON_ACTIO 197     233     86766811 frmweb@srfoapd 6(X) 0( ) TX
      NS                                        04 (TNS V1-V3)

APPS  BEN_BATCH_RANGES 197     233     86766811 frmweb@srfoapd 6(X) 0( ) TX
                                                   04 (TNS V1-V3)

APPS  BEN_ELIG_DPNT    197     233     86766811 frmweb@srfoapd 6(X) 0( ) TX
                                                   04 (TNS V1-V3)

APPS  BEN_PTNL_LER_FOR 197     233     86766811 frmweb@srfoapd 6(X) 0( ) TX
      _PER                                      04 (TNS V1-V3)

APPS  BEN_PRTT_ENRT_AC 197     233     86766811 frmweb@srfoapd 6(X) 0( ) TX
      TN_F                                      04 (TNS V1-V3)

APPS  BEN_PIL_ELCTBL_C 197     233     86766811 frmweb@srfoapd 6(X) 0( ) TX
      HC_POPL                                   04 (TNS V1-V3)

APPS  BEN_PER_IN_LER   197     233     86766811 frmweb@srfoapd 6(X) 0( ) TX
                                                   04 (TNS V1-V3)

APPS  FND_SESSIONS     197     233     86766811 frmweb@srfoapd 6(X) 0( ) TX
                                                   04 (TNS V1-V3)

APPS  BEN_ENRT_RT      197     233     86766811 frmweb@srfoapd 6(X) 0( ) TX
                                                   04 (TNS V1-V3)

APPS  BEN_ENRT_BNFT    197     233     86766811 frmweb@srfoapd 6(X) 0( ) TX
                                                   04 (TNS V1-V3)

APPS  BEN_ELIG_PER_OPT 197     233     86766811 frmweb@srfoapd 6(X) 0( ) TX
      _F                                        04 (TNS V1-V3)

APPS  BEN_ELIG_PER_F   197     233     86766811 frmweb@srfoapd 6(X) 0( ) TX
                                                   04 (TNS V1-V3)

APPS  BEN_ELIG_PER_ELC 197     233     86766811 frmweb@srfoapd 6(X) 0( ) TX
      TBL_CHC                                   04 (TNS V1-V3)

APPS  BEN_BENEFIT_ACTI 197     233     86766811 frmweb@srfoapd 6(X) 0( ) TX
      ONS                                       04 (TNS V1-V3)
```

WHAT PERFORMANCE SCRIPTS (continued)

WHAT SQL ID AND (M.BARONE) (DBTIER: EXECUTES USING -- SQLPLUS / AS SYSDBA)

WHAT SQL PLAN (M.BARONE)

Use **whatsqlid** and **whatsqlplan** to quickly create an accurate SQL-Execution-Plan showing the SQL-Performance and the SQL-Cost-Based-Optimization. **whatsqlid** and **whatsqlplan** can be executed while the SQL is executing or several days AFTER the SQL has completed.

Normally the SQL-History can warehouse SQL-Statements for a full day or more. Once the **sqlid** is identified, then the **whatsqlplan** script is executed.

- **whatsqlid** searches SQL-History for TableName/Index/SQL-Statement, etc.
- **whatsqlid** searches SQL-History for any recently executed SQL-Statement.
- **whatsqlplan** displays the **SQL-Explain-Plan** on the executed **SQL.**

Example: whatsqlid

```
19-JUN-14                 OATC (oratest) SQLText SQLID
14:54:04

LastActive
Date Time   SQL Hash-ID
----------- --------------
20-JUN-14   55dc767ajydh3
18:58:48
```

Example: whatsqlplan

```
                       OATC (oratest) SQLText SQLID

PLAN_TABLE_OUTPUT
------------------------------------------------------------------------
SQL_ID  55dc767ajydh3, child number 0
------------------------------------
SELECT PROFILE_OPTION_VALUE FROM FND_PROFILE_OPTION_VALUES WHERE
PROFILE_OPTION_ID = :B4 AND APPLICATION_ID = :B3 AND LEVEL_ID = 10003
AND LEVEL_VALUE = :B2 AND LEVEL_VALUE_APPLICATION_ID = :B1 AND
PROFILE_OPTION_VALUE IS NOT NULL

Plan hash value: 2802907561

| Id | Operation               | Name                         |Rows|Bytes|Cost (%CPU)| Time     |
---------------------------------------------------------------------------------------------------
|   0 |SELECT STATEMENT        |                              |    |     |    3 (100)|          |
|*  1 | TABLE ACCESS BY INDEX|FND_PROFILE_OPTION_VALUES      |  1 |  25 |    3    (0)| 00:00:01 |
|*  2 |  INDEX RANGE SCAN      |FND_PROFILE_OPTION_VALUES_U1  |  1 |     |    2    (0)| 00:00:01 |
---------------------------------------------------------------------------------------------------

Predicate Information (identified by operation id):
---------------------------------------------------
   1 - filter("PROFILE_OPTION_VALUE" IS NOT NULL)
   2 - access("APPLICATION_ID"=:B3 AND "PROFILE_OPTION_ID"=:B4 AND "LEVEL_ID"=10003 AND
              "LEVEL_VALUE"=:B2 AND "LEVEL_VALUE_APPLICATION_ID"=:B1)
```

Chapter 6 – "What Performance Tracing"

What Performance Tracing – What Are They All About?

The "what performance tracing" is a series of operating system level scripts that interrogate the Oracle E-Business Suiteinternal tables for information not easily obtained through other means. These scripts were created to provide information quickly, accurately, and in an easy to read format.

The "what performance tracing" are designed to assist System Administrators, Database Administrators, or really any IS/IT personnel looking for specific information such as what-forms-are-performing-poorly, and what-user-Apache-Errors are associated with what Client-PC-Connections, etc. There are a wide variety of scripts found within this book. Please review the table of contents and appendixes to find a "what" script that best meets your needs.

WHAT PERFORMANCE TRACING (continued)
WHOSUP + UNIX-COMMANDS (M.BARONE)

Use **whosup** and **Unix/Linux/AIX Commands** to quickly navigate all the way from the ClientPC to the AppsTier and display the Apache-Errors associated with the ClientPC.

whosup

```
#-----------------------------------------------------------------#
#- ICX Connections (whosup)                                      -#
#-----------------------------------------------------------------#
10-SEP-13                     Apps ICX Connections
13:18:36                       Sorted by UserName
                                                                       Last
                                                              ICX      ICX
UserName User Description   Responsibility                 Connect  Activity
-------- ------------------ ----------------------------- --------- --------
94813    Carpenter, Mr. Ken US Super HRMS Manager          10-SEP-13 10-SEP-13
                                                           11:01:52  11:06:59

#-----------------------------------------------------------------#
#- Forms Connections (whosup)                                    -#
#-----------------------------------------------------------------#
10-SEP-13                       Apps FormServer
13:18:37                       Sorted by UserName

                   Apps                               Apps     Apps        Form
                   Short                   FormStart  Server   Server    Server
User   FormName    Name  Responsibility Time      ProcID   Name      AUDSID
------ ----------- ----- -------------- --------- -------- ------- ---------
94813  Authenticat BEN   US Super HRMS  10-SEP-13 29229254 srfoapd  86766811
       the person         Manager        11:06:45           04
```

WHAT PERFORMANCE TRACING (continued)
WHOSUP + UNIX-COMMANDS (M.BARONE)

Use **whosup** and **Unix/Linux/AIX Commands** to quickly navigate all the way from the ClientPC to the AppsTier and display the Apache-Errors associated with the ClientPC.

AppsTier/FormServerTier: Unix/Linux/AIX
Use the Unix/Linux/AIX Command **ps -efa | grep frmweb**
to quickly list the AppsTier/FormServerTier FormWeb Sessions.

The AppsTier/FormServer Tier FormWeb also shows the **PC-Client IP-Address.**

[UNIX/Linux/AIX]:
ps -efa | grep frmweb

```
applmgr 261490 2148 frmweb server webfile=HTTP-,0,1,default,10.20.100.127
```

[UNIX/Linux/AIX]
grep 10.20.100.127 $LOG_HOME/ora/10.1.3/Apache/*error.log

```
[Tue Nov 12 07:16:55 2013] [error] [client 10.20.100.127] [ecid:
13842586:10.1] mod_oc4j: Failed to find a failover oc4j process for
session request for destination: application://oacore (no island or jgroup).

[Tue Nov 12 07:21:57 2013] [warn] [client 10.20.100.127]
oc4j_socket_recvfull ti med out
```

WHAT PERFORMANCE TRACING (continued)
WHOSUP + UNIX-COMMANDS (M.BARONE)

Use **whosup** and **Unix/Linux/AIX Commands** to quickly navigate all the way from the ClientPC to the AppsTier and display the Apache-Errors associated with the ClientPC.

Also Note: A Desktop PC can be used to determine the User's Neme from the IPAddress

Start

Search Programs and Files

Type **CMD** **in the Search Programs and Files Box**

```
c:\>nslookup 10.20.100.127
Server:   oatc.oatcinc.com
Address:   10.10.10.10

Name:     oatc.oatcinc.com
Address:   10.20.100.127

Name:     mbarone.oatc.oatcinc.com
Address:   10.20.100.127
```

In the Command) Window, type. **nslookup XXX.XXX.XXX.XXX**

Where ###.###.###.### is the
IPAddress from the Unix/Linux Screen (above).

Example: **nslookup 10.20.100.127**

Chapter 7 – "What Patch Scripts"

WHAT PATCH SCRIPTS – WHAT ARE THEY ALL ABOUT?

The "what patch scripts" are a series of operating system level scripts that interrogate the Oracle E-Business Suiteinternal tables for information not easily obtained through other means. These scripts were created to provide information quickly, accurately, and in an easy to read format.

The "what patch scripts" are designed to assist System Administrators, Database Administrators, or really any IS/IT personnel looking for specific information such as what-patches-have-been-applied, and what-patches-were-applied-on-which-Server and what-patch-details-and-times. There are a wide variety of scripts found within this book. Please review the table of contents and appendixes to find a "what" script that best meets your needs.

WHAT PATCH SCRIPTS (continued)

WHAT PATCH NODE (M.BARONE)

- What E-Business Suite Nodes are Updated by this Patch?

If Your E-Business Suite Environment has MORE-THAN-ONE AppsTier-Node, and you are NOT using a SHARED FILE SYSTEM between the AppsTier Nodes, then this Script will help determine if patches have been applied on ANY/ALL of the AppsTier Nodes.

Example:

```
#----------------------------------------------------------------#
#- What Patch Nodes Were Patched by Patch (whatpatchnode)       -#
#----------------------------------------------------------------#

              OATC (oratest) Apps What Patch Modules
          EBusiness Patch 16052604 Updated These Server/Nodes

AD_Bugs  Node                           Patch                Patch
Patch    Patch                          Creation             LastUpdate
Number   Number   Node Name             Date                 Date
-------- -------- ------------- -------------------- --------------------
16052604 16052604 oatcapd04     18-MAY-2014 01:35:30 18-MAY-2014 01:35:30
```

WHAT PATCH SCRIPTS (continued)

WHAT PATCH MODULE (M.BARONE)

- What E-Business Suite Modules/Products were Updated by this Patch?

Example:

```
#-----------------------------------------------------------------#
#- What Patch Modules Were Updated by Patch (whatpatchmodules) -#
#-----------------------------------------------------------------#

                 OATC (oratest) Apps What Patch Modules
             EBusiness Patch 16052604 Updated These Products

Product
ShortName
------------------------------
iby
```

WHAT PATCH SCRIPTS (continued)

WHAT PATCH DETAIL (M.BARONE)

- What E-Business Suite Patch Details (Parent and Included Patches) were applied AFTER a speficied date?

Example:

```
#-----------------------------------------------------------------#
#- whatpatchdetail:                                              -#
#-----------------------------------------------------------------#

23-MAY-14        OATC (oratest) Apps eBusiness Patch Summary
20:17:33               EBusiness Patches Sorted by Date

                                      Bug     ARU
Patch                       Patch    Abbrev  Release
Date                        Number   iation  Name
--------------------        -------- ------- -------
10-MAY-2012 00:32:08 10197697 fnd     R12
10-MAY-2012 00:32:14 10051072 fnd     R12
10-MAY-2012 00:32:14 9198540  fnd     R12
11-MAY-2012 01:07:15 8668357  frm     R12
14-MAY-2012 19:23:57 12728634 sqlap   R12
14-MAY-2012 19:29:20 14559297 pjc     R12
14-MAY-2012 19:29:20 11804121 pjc     R12
16-MAY-2012 22:48:16 12747567 frm     R12
16-MAY-2012 22:48:17 10136174 frm     R12
```

CHAPTER 8 – "E-BUSINESS12.1 TECHSTACK"

E-Business Suite 12.1 TechStack (Application Code Stack)
E-Business Suite 12.1 TechStack (Database Tier Code Stack)

WHAT COMPILE PLL (M.BARONE)

- What E-Business Suite Compile – Program Link Library (PLL)

Example: Compile the CUSTOM.pll

```
#--------------------------------------------------------------#
#- AppsTier Connection   whatcompile_pll                      -#
#--------------------------------------------------------------#

Forms 10.1 (Form Compiler) Version 10.1.2.3.0 (Production)
Forms 10.1 (Form Compiler): Release  - Production

Copyright (c) 1982, 2005, Oracle.  All rights reserved.

Oracle Database 11g Enterprise Edition Release 11.2.0.3.0 - 64bit
Production
     With the Partitioning, OLAP, Data Mining and Real Application
Testing options
PL/SQL Version 10.1.0.5.0 (Production)
Oracle Procedure Builder V10.1.2.3.0 - Production
Oracle Virtual Graphics System Version 10.1.2.0.0 (Production)
Oracle Multimedia Version 10.1.2.0.2 (Production)
Oracle Tools Integration Version 10.1.2.0.2 (Production)
Oracle Tools Common Area Version 10.1.2.0.2
Oracle CORE     10.1.0.5.0      Production
Compiling library CUSTOM...
  Invalidating Package Spec CUSTOM......
  Invalidating Package Body CUSTOM......
  Compiling Package Spec CUSTOM......
  Compiling Package Body CUSTOM......
 Done.

/d121/app/121/appl/au/12.0.0/resource/CUSTOM.pll
/d121/app/121/appl/au/12.0.0/resource/CUSTOM.plx
```

E-Business Suite 12.1 TechStack (Application Code Stack)
E-Business Suite 12.1 TechStack (Database Tier Code Stack)

WHAT COMPILE FORM (M.BARONE)

- What E-Business Suite Compile -- Form

Example: Compile the FNDSCSGN.fmb

```
#-----------------------------------------------------------------#
#- AppsTier Connection  whatcompile_form                         -#
#-----------------------------------------------------------------#

Forms 10.1 (Form Compiler) Version 10.1.2.3.0 (Production)
Forms 10.1 (Form Compiler): Release  - Production
Copyright (c) 1982, 2005, Oracle.  All rights reserved.

Oracle Database 11g Enterprise Edition Release 11.2.0.3.0 - 64bit
Production
     With the Partitioning, OLAP, Data Mining and Real Application
Testing options
PL/SQL Version 10.1.0.5.0 (Production)
Oracle Procedure Builder V10.1.2.3.0 - Production
Oracle Virtual Graphics System Version 10.1.2.0.0 (Production)
Oracle Multimedia Version 10.1.2.0.2 (Production)
Oracle Tools Integration Version 10.1.2.0.2 (Production)
Oracle Tools Common Area Version 10.1.2.0.2
Oracle CORE     10.1.0.5.0      Production
.
.
.

Compiling WHEN-BUTTON-PRESSED trigger on CANCEL_PROPERTIES item in
PROGRESS_INDICATOR data block...
   No compilation errors.

Compiling WHEN-MOUSE-UP trigger in FOLDER_PROMPT_MULTIROW property
class...
   No compilation errors.

Compiling WHEN-BUTTON-PRESSED trigger in FOLDER_OPEN property
class...
   No compilation errors.

Created form file
/d121/app/121/appl/po/12.0.0/forms/US/FNDSCSGN.fmx
```

CHAPTER 9 – "E-BUSINESS12.2 TECHSTACK"

E-Business Suite 12.2 TechStack (Application Code Stack)
E-Business Suite 12.2 TechStack (Database Tier Code Stack)

WHAT COMPILE PLL (M.BARONE)

- What E-Business Suite Compile – Program Link Library (PLL)

Example: Compile the CUSTOM.pll

```
#----------------------------------------------------------------#
#- AppsTier Connection  whatcompile_pll                          -#
#----------------------------------------------------------------#

Forms 10.1 (Form Compiler) Version 10.1.2.3.0 (Production)
Forms 10.1 (Form Compiler): Release  - Production

Copyright (c) 1982, 2005, Oracle.  All rights reserved.

Oracle Database 11g Enterprise Edition Release 11.2.0.3.0 - 64bit
Production
     With the Partitioning, OLAP, Data Mining and Real Application
Testing options
PL/SQL Version 10.1.0.5.0 (Production)
Oracle Procedure Builder V10.1.2.3.0 - Production
Oracle Virtual Graphics System Version 10.1.2.0.0 (Production)
Oracle Multimedia Version 10.1.2.0.2 (Production)
Oracle Tools Integration Version 10.1.2.0.2 (Production)
Oracle Tools Common Area Version 10.1.2.0.2
Oracle CORE     10.1.0.5.0      Production
Compiling library CUSTOM...
  Invalidating Package Spec CUSTOM......
  Invalidating Package Body CUSTOM......
  Compiling Package Spec CUSTOM......
  Compiling Package Body CUSTOM......
 Done.

/d121/app/122/appl/au/12.0.0/resource/CUSTOM.pll
/d121/app/122/appl/au/12.0.0/resource/CUSTOM.plx
```

E-Business Suite 12.2 TechStack (Application Code Stack)
E-Business Suite 12.2 TechStack (Database Tier Code Stack)

WHAT COMPILE FORM (M.BARONE)

- What E-Business Suite Compile -- Form

Example: Compile the FNDSCSGN.fmb

```
#-----------------------------------------------------------------#
#- AppsTier Connection  whatcompile_form                        -#
#-----------------------------------------------------------------#

Forms 10.1 (Form Compiler) Version 10.1.2.3.0 (Production)
Forms 10.1 (Form Compiler): Release  - Production
Copyright (c) 1982, 2005, Oracle.  All rights reserved.

Oracle Database 11g Enterprise Edition Release 11.2.0.3.0 - 64bit
With the Partitioning, OLAP, Data Mining and Real Application
Testing options

PL/SQL Version 10.1.0.5.0 (Production)
Oracle Procedure Builder V10.1.2.3.0 - Production
Oracle Virtual Graphics System Version 10.1.2.0.0 (Production)
Oracle Multimedia Version 10.1.2.0.2 (Production)
Oracle Tools Integration Version 10.1.2.0.2 (Production)
Oracle Tools Common Area Version 10.1.2.0.2
Oracle CORE     10.1.0.5.0      Production
.
.
.

Compiling WHEN-BUTTON-PRESSED trigger on CANCEL_PROPERTIES item in
PROGRESS_INDICATOR data block...
   No compilation errors.

Compiling WHEN-MOUSE-UP trigger in FOLDER_PROMPT_MULTIROW property
class...
   No compilation errors.

Compiling WHEN-BUTTON-PRESSED trigger in FOLDER_OPEN property
class...
   No compilation errors.

Created form file
/d121/app/121/appl/po/12.0.0/forms/US/FNDSCSGN.fmx
```

CHAPTER 10 – "E-BUSINESS11I TECHSTACK LOGS"

- **E-Business Suite 11i TechStack Log/Debug Files**
- **Use the following Outline to help locate your Log/Debug File**

Environment-Variable Name: $APACHE_TOP
cd $APACHE_TOP/Apache/logs

Apache: **$IAS_ORACLE_HOME/Apache/Apache/logs**
error_log.1373932800
access_log.1373932800

Apache XML Configuration Files: **$IAS_ORACLE_HOME/Apache/Apache/logs**
$ORACLE_HOME/Apache/Apache/conf
access.conf
apps.conf
custom_apache.conf
httpd.conf
mime.types
oracle_apache.conf
trusted.conf
url_fw.conf
server.xml

Chapter 11 – "E-Business12.1 TechStack Logs"

- **E-Business Suite 12.1 TechStack Log/Debug Files**
- **Use the following Outline to help locate your Log/Debug File**

Environment-Variable Name: $LOG_HOME
cd $LOG_HOME ($INST_TOP/apps/<SID-Name>_<Server-Name>/logs)

```
Apache:                 ./ora/10.1.3/Apache
   error_log.1373932800
   access_log.1373932800

j2ee                    ./ora/10.1.3/j2ee
   forms
      ./forms/forms_default_group_1:
         application.log
         global-application.log
         jms.log
         log.xml
         rmi.log
         server.log
         system-application.log
   oacore
      oacore_default_group_1
         application.log
         global-application.log
         jms.log
         log.xml
         rmi.log
         server.log
         system-application.log
   oafm
      oafm_default_group_1
         application.log
         ascontrol-application.log
         global-application.log
         jms.log
         log.xml
         mapviewer-application.log
         rmi.log
         server.log
         system-application.log

javacache               ./ora/10.1.3/javacache

opmn                    ./ora/10.1.3/opmn
   HTTP_Server~1.log
      default_group~forms~default_group~1.log
      default_group~oacore~default_group~1.log
      default_group~oafm~default_group~1.log
      opmn.dbg
      opmn.log
      opmn.out
```

CHAPTER 12 – "E-BUSINESS12.2 TECHSTACK LOGS"

- **E-Business Suite 12.2 TechStack Log/Debug Files**
- **Use the following Outline to help locate your Log/Debug File**

adop (OnLine Patching) Logs
$NE_BASE/EBSapps/log/adop/<adop_session>/<phase>_<date>_<time>/<context_name>/log

Online Patching Filesystem Cloning Logs:
$INST_TOP/admin/log

Autoconfig Logs
AppsTier: $INST_TOP/admin/log/<MMDDhhmm>
DBTier: $ORACLE_HOME/appsutil/log/<CONTEXT_NAME>/<MMDDhhmm>

$ADMIN_SCRIPTS_HOME Startup / Shutdown
oacore,
forms,
apache,
opmn,
weblogic
admin

$LOG_HOME/appl/admin/log

Concurrent Manager / Concurrent Request Log/Out
Log files: $APPLCSF/$APPLLOG ($NE_BASE/inst/<CONTEXT_NAME>/logs/appl/conc/log)
Out files: $APPLCSF/$APPLOUT ($NE_BASE/inst/<CONTEXT_NAME>/logs/appl/conc/out)

OPMN, HTTP, Access and OHS Log Files and DeBug Files
$IAS_ORACLE_HOME/instances/<ohs_instance>/diagnostics/logs

Weblogic Node Manager
$FMW_HOME/wlserver_10.3/common/nodemanager/nmHome1/nodemanager.log

Weblogic Oracle Management Service Log
$EBS_DOMAIN_HOME/sysman/log

Weblogic Logs
$EBS_DOMAIN_HOME/servers/<server_name>/logs/<server_name>.out

Environment-Variable Name: $LOG_HOME
cd $LOG_HOME ($INST_TOP/apps/<SID-Name>_<Server-Name>/logs)

```
Apache
   error_log.1373932800
   access_log.1373932800

j2ee
   forms
      ./forms/forms_default_group_1:
         application.log
         global-application.log
         jms.log
         log.xml
         rmi.log
         server.log
         system-application.log
   oacore
      oacore_default_group_1
         application.log
         global-application.log
         jms.log
         log.xml
         rmi.log
         server.log
         system-application.log
   oafm
      oafm_default_group_1
         application.log
         ascontrol-application.log
         global-application.log
         jms.log
         log.xml
         mapviewer-application.log
         rmi.log
         server.log
         system-application.log

javacache

opmn
   HTTP_Server~1.log
      default_group~forms~default_group~1.log
      default_group~oacore~default_group~1.log
      default_group~oafm~default_group~1.log
      opmn.dbg
      opmn.log
      opmn.out
```

CHAPTER 13 – "WHAT FUNCTIONAL SCRIPTS"

WHAT FUNCTIONAL SCRIPTS – WHAT ARE THEY ALL ABOUT?

The "what Functional scripts" are a series of operating system level scripts that interrogate the Oracle E-Business Suite internal tables for information not easily obtained through other means. These scripts were created to provide information quickly, accurately, and in an easy to read format.

The "what Functional scripts" are designed to assist System Administrators, Database Administrators, or really any IS/IT personnel looking for specific information such as what-accounting-periods, and what-account-period-is-open and what-organization-names. There are a wide variety of scripts found within this book. Please review the table of contents and appendixes to find a "what" script that best meets your needs.

WHAT FUNCTIONAL SCRIPTS (continued)

WHAT ORG ID (M.BARONE)

- What E-Business Suite Organization IDs and Names have been defined?

The E-Business Suite Organizations (ORG_ID) governs the USERs ability to see and query Organizatal Data and Financial Information. This SQL-Script displays all of the defined E-Business Suite Organizations (ORG_IDs).

Example:

```
#--------------------------------------------------------------#
#- What ORGID(whatorgid)                                      -#
#--------------------------------------------------------------#

10-May-14      appc (oatc.oatcinc.com) Apps Organization Names
16:31:31            eBusiness 11i/12 ORG_ID and Organizations

Organization ID Organization Name
--------------- ----------------------------------------
              0 Oracle Application Technical Consultants
             10 OATC, Inc.
```

WHAT FUNCTIONAL SCRIPTS (continued)

WHAT SET OF BOOKS (M.BARONE)

- What E-Business Suite Accounting Set Of Books (SOB) Period Statuses.

The E-Business Suite Functional Accounting Set of Books (SOB) and Set of Books Period-Statuses Summary for the Set of Books (Open, Closed, Future, Never).

Example:

```
#-----------------------------------------------------------------#
#- Whatsob (whatsob)                                             -#
#-----------------------------------------------------------------#

01-APR-15          E-Business Suite Set Of Book              Page:    1
02:26:50         whatsetofbooks -- Sorted by SetOfBooks ID

  Set
   Of
  Bks Period          GL Period                                    GL SOB   Co-
   ID Set Name        Name                 GL Description          Status   unt
----- --------------- -------------------- --------------------   ------- ----
 2021 OATC_12MONTHS   OATC & Affiliates                            Closed    71
      OATC_12MONTHS   OATC & Affiliates                            Future     1
      OATC_12MONTHS   OATC & Affiliates                            Never    211
      OATC_12MONTHS   OATC & Affiliates                            Open      16

 2024 OATCinc        OATCinc                                       Never     52
```

WHAT FUNCTIONAL SCRIPTS (continued)

WHAT SET OF BOOKS (M.BARONE)

- What E-Business Suite Accounting Set Of Books (SOB) Period Details.

The E-Business Suite Functional Accounting Set of Books (SOB) and Set of Books Period-Statuses (Open, Closed, Future, Never, etc) detail counts.

Example:

```
#------------------------------------------------------#
# whatsob_periods:  Oracle Apps Set Of Books Periods    #
#------------------------------------------------------#

01-APR-15     E-Business Suite Set Of Books - Periods              Page:    1
02:58:01     whatsob_periods -- Set Of Books - Periods

GL Period Name
YY-MM                GL Period Status    GL Period Count
-------------------- -------------------- ---------------
14-08                Never                              3
14-09                Closed                             1
14-10                Never                              2
14-10                Closed                             1
14-10                Never                              2
14-11                Closed                             1
14-11                Never                              1
14-12                Open                               1
.
.
.
```

WHAT FUNCTIONAL SCRIPTS (continued)

WHAT CURRENCY (M.BARONE)

- What E-Business Suite Currency/Currencies have been defined?

The E-Business Suite Currencies governs the Financial Currencies that can be used in E-Business Suite Transactions. This SQL-Script displays the E-Business Suite Currency and whether the E-Business Suite can transact in Multiple Currencies.

Example:

```
#---------------------------------------------------------------#
#- What (whatcurrency)                                         -#
#---------------------------------------------------------------#

10-May-14      appc (oatc.oatcinc.com) Currency Information
17:14:36             eBusiness 11i/12 Currency Information

                                        Currency
Currency Code                           Symbol
---------------------------------------- ----------
STAT
USD                                     $

Multiple Currencies: No
```

WHAT FUNCTIONAL SCRIPTS (continued)

WHAT CUSTOM APPS (M.BARONE)

- What E-Business Suite Custom Applications have been Registered.

The E-Business Suite Custom Applications are registered and used to implement Custom Applications.

Example:

```
#---------------------------------------------------------------#
#- What (whatcustomapps)                                       -#
#---------------------------------------------------------------#

10-May-14      appc (oatc.oatcinc.com) Custom Applications
17:37:50              eBusiness 11i/12 Custom Applications

    ID Short Name                     BasePath
------ ------------------------------ ------------
 20003 GLCUST                         GLCUST_TOP
 20023 ARCUST                         ARCUST_TOP
 20024 POCUST                         POCUST_TOP
 20043 APCUST                         APCUST_TOP
```

WHAT FUNCTIONAL SCRIPTS (continued)

WHAT FNDLOBS USER (M.BARONE)

- What E-Business Suite Users are Storing/Saving FND-Attachements.

E-Business Suite FND_Attachements and FND_LOBS (Long Objects) are very difficult to manage, clean, maintain. Removing OLD/Purged FND_LOBS Attachements resures Functional User to Purge/Delete the FND_Attachement, then launch the Concurrent Request: *Purge Concurrent Request and/or Manager Data.*

Once the *Purge Concurrent Request and/or Manager Data* Concurrent Request completes, the FND_LOBS space can be re-Claimed.

```
sqlplus  APPS
   ALTER TABLE fnd_lobs MODIFY LOB (file_data) (SHRINK SPACE);
```

Example:

```
#-----------------------------------------------------------------#
#- E-Business (whatfndlob_user)                                  -#
#-----------------------------------------------------------------#

31-AUG-16     OATCinc1 (oatcinc1.oatcinc.com) FND_LOBS Objects
08:38:21                         Sorted by UserName

                                      FND
User              FND_LOBS      Document FND_LOBS         FND_LOBS   FND_LOBS
Name              CreatedDate         ID File Name        Size(Mb)   Description
---------------- ------------- --------- ---------------- ---------- -----------
Barone, Michael   23-MAY-2016     319859
Barone, Michael   14-MAY-2016     318873
Barone, Michael   13-MAY-2016     318871
```

WHAT FUNCTIONAL SCRIPTS (continued)

WHAT FNDLOBS EXTENTS (M.BARONE)

- What E-Business Suite Users are Storing/Saving FND-Attachements.

E-Business Suite FND_Attachements and FND_LOBS (Long Objects) are very difficult to manage, clean, maintain. Removing OLD/Purged FND_LOBS Attachements resures Functional User to Purge/Delete the FND_Attachement, then launch the Concurrent Request: *Purge Concurrent Request and/or Manager Data.*

Once the *Purge Concurrent Request and/or Manager Data* Concurrent Request completes, the FND_LOBS space can be re-Claimed.

```
sqlplus  APPS
   ALTER TABLE fnd_lobs MODIFY LOB (file_data) (SHRINK SPACE);
```

Example:

```
#------------------------------------------------------------------#
#- E-Business (whatfndlob_extents)                                -#
#------------------------------------------------------------------#

31-AUG-16      OATCincl  (oatcincl.oatcinc.com) FND_LOBS Extents
08:38:21             Sorted by Segment_Name, Segment_ID
                                                                          Extent
                                                                           Bytes
SEGMENT NAME                 SEGMENT TYPE         EXTENT-ID      BYTES  Size(Mb)
---------------------------  -----------------  ---------  ---------- ---------
SYS_LOB0000239111C00014$$    LOBSEGMENT                 0      131072     21474
SYS_LOB0000239111C00014$$    LOBSEGMENT                 1      131072     21474
SYS_LOB0000239111C00014$$    LOBSEGMENT                 2      131072     21474

. . .

SYS_LOB0000239111C00014$$   LOBSEGMENT             171786      131072     21474
SYS_LOB0000239111C00014$$   LOBSEGMENT             171787      131072     21474
SYS_LOB0000239111C00014$$   LOBSEGMENT             171788      131072     21474
SYS_LOB0000239111C00014$$   LOBSEGMENT             171789      131072     21474
```

Chapter 14 – "What WorkFlow Scripts"

what WorkFlow scripts – what are they all about?

The "what WorkFlow scripts" are a series of operating system level scripts that interrogate the Oracle E-Business Suite internal tables for information not easily obtained through other means. These scripts were created to provide information quickly, accurately, and in an easy to read format.

The "what WorkFlow scripts" are designed to assist System Administrators, Database Administrators, or really any IS/IT personnel looking for specific information such as what-worflow-summary, and what-workflow-detail. There are a wide variety of scripts found within this book. Please review the table of contents and appendixes to find a "what" script that best meets your needs.

WHAT WORKFLOW SCRIPTS (continued)

WHATS UP (M.BARONE)

- What E-Business Suite Services are UP? Workflow Services are UP ?
- What E-Business Suite AppsTier/DBTier/Workflow Services are Available?

Use this Script to quickly determine which E-Business Suite DBTier and AppsTier Sevices are UP/DOWN When AppsTier/DBTier/Workflow Services are DOWN the Script shows “No” under the appropriate heading.

Example: AppsTier Services are UP. DBTier Services are UP.

```
            oratest.oatcinc.com Apps-11i/12.1 Survey

            A p p l i c a t i o n       D a t a b a s e
               S e r v i c e s          S e r v i c e s
               --  Apache  --  App      App 11g 11g
Apps      Frm Svr Svr Svr JRE DB       Cnc DB  Ora  WF-Java WF-Java
SIDs      Svr iAS PLS 920 Svr Lnr      Mgr Lsr DB   Server  AgntLst
--------- --- --- --- --- --- ---      --- --- ---  ------- -------
oatc      Yes Yes Yes Yes Yes Yes      Yes Yes Yes  Running Running

             Current Activity
             ------------------------------
             Forms-Connections:           9
             ConcReqs Running:            2

             Daily Activity
             ------------------------------
             Web-AppsLocalLogin Today:   20
```

WHAT WORKFLOW SCRIPTS (continued)

WHAT CONC QUEUE (M.BARONE)

- What Concurrent Manager Queues are ACTIVE/RUNNING?
- What Concurrent Managers are ENABLED/DISABLED?
- What Concurrent Managers are Fully Loaded/Backlogged/Idle?

Use this Script to quickly examine/compare different E-Business Suite Environments and find the Concurrent Managers that are too-busy or under-utilized. Also this Script shows whether the Concurrent-Manager is in Debug-Mode or has a Diagnostic-Level.

Example:

```
28-MAY-14                      EBusiness Concurrent Queues          Page:    1
17:14:40                  whatconcqueue -- Sorted by Queue-Name

Concurrent           Concurrent Queue      Conc   Conc   Conc Conc     Conc
Queue                Queue      Enable    Queue  Queue  Queue Queue    Diag
Description          Name       Disable     Max Runing Target Node     Lvl
-------------------- ---------- -------- ----- ------ ------ ------- ----
C AQCART Service     C_AQCT_SVC Enabled      0      0      1
CRP Inquiry Manager  CRPINQMGR  Enabled      0      0      2          N
Conflict Resolution  FNDCRM     Enabled      1      1      1          N
Manager

Debug Service        Debug_Serv Enabled      0      0      1
                     ice

FastFormula          FFTM       Enabled      0      0      1
Transaction Manager

Human Resources      HRM        Enabled      3      3      3          N

INV Remote Procedure INVTMRPM   Enabled      0      0      4
Manager

Internal Manager     FNDICM     Enabled      1      1      0          N
Internal Monitor:    FNDIM_ORAT Enabled      0      0      0 ORATEST
ORATEST              TEST

Inventory Manager    INVMGR     Enabled      1      1      1          N
KBACE                KBACE      Enabled      5      5      5          N
Labor Distribution   LDMSTD     Enabled      3      3      3          N
.
.
.
Standard Manager     STANDARD   Enabled     20     20     20          N

Workflow Mailer      WFMGSMD    Enabled      0      0      1
Workflow Mailer      WFMLRSVC   Enabled      1      1      1
Service

Workflow Summary     WFMGSMS    Enabled      0      0      1
Mailer
```

WHAT WORKFLOW SCRIPTS (continued)

WHAT WF (T.BLANFORD)

- What WorkFlow Services are ACTIVE/RUNNING?

Use this Script to quickly examine/compare different E-Business Suite Environments and find the status of the WorkFlow Services.

Example:

```
05-NOV-15            PROD (oatcinc) WorkFlow Services Summary         Page:    1
17:15:00                DBA WorkFlow Services Summary Report

WF Component Name                      Status
-------------------------------------- ----------
Workflow Notification Mailer           Up
Agent Listeners                        Down
Service Components                     Down
Workflow Background Process            Up
Workflow Control Queue Cleanup         Up
Workflow Work Items Statistics         Up
Concurrent Program

Workflow Mailer Statistics Concurrent  Up
Program

Workflow Agent Activity Statistics     Up
Concurrent Program

Purge Obsolete Workflow Runtime Data   Up
```

WHAT WORKFLOW SCRIPTS (continued)

WHAT WF DEFERRED (M.BARONE)

- What WorkFlow Deferred Process are ACTIVE/RETAINED?

Use this Script to quickly examine/compare different E-Business Suite Environments and find the status of the WorkFlow Deferred Processes.

Example:

```
05-NOV-15     PROD (oatcinc) WorkFlow Deferred Processes        Page:    1
18:36:07     DBA WorkFlow Deferred Processes Report

WorkFlow Desc (CORRID)                                    State        Count
-------------------------------------------------------- ------------ ------
APPS:oracle.apps.wf.notification.send                     Retained       142
APPS:oracle.apps.fnd.wf.ds.user.updated                   Retained         2
APPS:oracle.apps.wf.notification.cancel                   Retained         9
APPS:oracle.apps.wf.notification.denormalize              Retained        50
```

WHAT WORKFLOW SCRIPTS (continued)

WHAT WF MAIL TYPES (M.BARONE)

- What WorkFlow Mail/Notification Types and Counts ?

Use this Script to quickly examine/compare different E-Business Suite Environments and find the WorkFlow Mail/Notification Types and Counts.

Example:

```
05-NOV-15     PROD (oatcinc) WorkFlow Notification Type         Page:    1
18:39:46         DBA WorkFlow Notification Type Report

WF Notification Type                       COUNT(*)
---------------------------------------- ----------
APVRMDER                                        177
AZNF004                                           1
CS_MSGS                                          14
HRSFL                                           109
HRSSA                                           353
HXCEMP                                          146
POAPPRV                                       21153
POERROR                                          55
PORCPT                                           58
POREQCHA                                        221
PORPOCHA                                         18
REQAPPRV                                        860
WFERROR                                       21969
WFTESTS                                           6
```

WHAT WORKFLOW SCRIPTS (continued)

WHAT WF MAIL STATUS (M.BARONE)

- What WorkFlow Mail/Notification Status and Counts ?

Use this Script to quickly examine/compare different E-Business Suite Environments and find the WorkFlow Mail/Notification Statuses and Counts. This Script can also be used to interrogate NEWLY Cloned E-Business Suite Environments for possible Workflow Notifications that will be dispatched/sent as soon as the WorkFlow Mailer is started.

Example:

```
05-NOV-15     PROD (oatcinc) WorkFlow Mail Status        Page:    1
18:39:50         DBA WorkFlow Notification Mail Status Report


WF Mail Status                                     Count
--------------------------------------- --------
SENT                                              44,158
MAIL                                                  52
```

WHAT WORKFLOW SCRIPTS (continued)

WHAT WF MAILER DEBUG (WFMLRDBG) (M.BARONE)

- What WorkFlow Mailer Debug – Full List of WorkFlow Activity (Debug) ?

Use this Script to quickly examine/compare different E-Business Suite Environments and find the WorkFlow Mailer Debug.

Example:

TABLE OF CONTENTS

Notification Item Information

Notification Id	Message Type	Message Name	Fwk Content	Begin Date	End Date	Recipient Role	More Info Role	Status	Mail Status	Call back	Context

Notification Recipient Role Members

User Name	Display Name	Email Address	Notification Pref	Language	Territory	Orig Sys	Orig Sys Id	Installec

Notification Recipient Role Information

Role Name	Display Name	Email Address	Notification Pref	Launguage	Territory	Orig Sys	Orig Sys Id	Installec

Notification Recipient Routing Rules

Action	Begin Date	End Date	Message Type	Message Name	Action Argument	Name	Type	Value

Notification Message Attribute Values

Name	Display Name	Sequence	Type	Sub Type	Value Type	Value	Format

Notification Attribute Values

Name	Number Value	Date Value	Text Value

WF_DEFERRED Queue Status

Message Id	Message State	Consumer Name	Queue	Exception Queue	Retry Count	Event Name	Event Key	Enqueue Time

WF_ERROR Queue Status

Message Id	Message State	Consumer Name	Queue	Exception Queue	Retry Count	Event Name	Event Key	Error Message	Error Stack

WF_NOTIFICATION_OUT Queue Status

Message Id	Message State	Consumer Name	Queue	Exception Queue	Retry Count	Enqueue Time	Dequeue Time

WF_NOTIFICATION_IN Queue Status

Message Id	Message State	Consumer Name	Queue	Exception Queue	Retry Count	Enqueue Time	Dequeue Time

WHAT WORKFLOW SCRIPTS (continued)

what wf mailer debug (wfmlrdbg) (M.Barone) (Continued)

Generate Notification Message

Notification Message in XML format	Time Taken to complete Generate: .12 Second

Content from WF_NOTIFICATION_OUT

Notification Message from WF_NOTIFICATION_OUT

Content from WF_NOTIFICATION_IN

Notification Message from WF_NOTIFICATION_IN

Profile Option Values

Parameter Name	Parameter Value

GSC WF_MAILER Component Parameters

Component Id	10011
Component Name	Workflow Notification Mailer
Component Status	RUNNING
Startup Mode	AUTOMATIC
Inbound Agent Name	WF_NOTIFICATION_IN
Outbound Agent Name	WF_NOTIFICATION_OUT
Correlation Id	

Date notification was sent

Parameter Name	Parameter Value	Parameter Description	Default Value

GSC WF_MAILER Component Scheduled Events

Component Id	10011
Component Name	Workflow Notification Mailer
Component Status	RUNNING

Request Id	Job Id	Event Name	Event Params	Event Frequency	What	Last Date	Last Scheduled

Workflow Notification Tags Value

Name	Tag ID	Action	Pattern	Reload

CHAPTER 15 – "WHAT OPERATING SYSTEM SCRIPTS"

WHAT OPERATING SYSTEM (OS) SCRIPTS – WHAT ARE THEY ALL ABOUT?

The "what OS scripts" are a series of operating system level scripts that interrogate the Unix/Linx Operating System (OS). These scripts were created to provide information quickly, accurately, and in an easy to read format.

The "what Operating System scripts" are designed to assist System Administrators, Database Administrators, or really any IS/IT personnel looking for specific information such as what-CPU-information, and what-RPM-Information. There are a wide variety of scripts found within this book. Please review the table of contents and appendixes to find a "what" script that best meets your needs.

WHAT OPERATING SYSTEM SCRIPTS (continued)

WHATS CPU (M.BARONE)

- What Operating System CPU (CPU-Count and CPU-Speed) ?

Use this Script to quickly determine the Unix/Linux Operating System CPU count sn CPU Speed.

Example: AppsTier or DBTier CPU Count and CPU Speed

```
#---------------------------------------------------------#
# whatcpu:                    Linux CPU and Memory Usage #
#---------------------------------------------------------#
processor         : 0
vendor_id         : GenuineIntel
cpu family        : 6
model             : 37
model name        : Intel(R) Xeon(R) CPU E7- 2830  @ 2.13GHz
stepping : 1
cpu MHz           : 2130.545
cache size        : 24576 KB
fdiv_bug : no
hlt_bug           : no
f00f_bug : no
coma_bug : no
fpu               : yes
fpu_exception     : yes
cpuid level       : 11
wp                : yes
flags             : fpu vme de pse tsc msr pae mce cx8 apic sep mtrr pge mca
cmov pat pse36 clflush dts acpi mmx fxsr sse sse2 ss nx rdtscp lm
constant_tsc ida nonstop_tsc arat pni ssse3 cx16 sse4_1 sse4_2 popcnt lahf_lm
[8]
bogomips : 4261.09

processor         : 1
vendor_id         : GenuineIntel
cpu family        : 6
model             : 37
model name        : Intel(R) Xeon(R) CPU E7- 2830  @ 2.13GHz
stepping : 1
cpu MHz           : 2130.545
cache size        : 24576 KB
fdiv_bug : no
hlt_bug           : no
f00f_bug : no
coma_bug : no
fpu               : yes
fpu_exception     : yes
cpuid level       : 11
wp                : yes
flags             : fpu vme de pse tsc msr pae mce cx8 apic sep mtrr pge mca
cmov pat pse36 clflush dts acpi mmx fxsr sse sse2 ss nx rdtscp lm
constant_tsc ida nonstop_tsc arat pni ssse3 cx16 sse4_1 sse4_2 popcnt lahf_lm
[8]
bogomips : 4261.00
```

WHAT OPERATING SYSTEM SCRIPTS (continued)

WHATS RPM (M.BARONE)

- What Operating System RPM (Redhat Package Manager) Information ?

Use this Script to quickly determine the Unix/Linux Operating System RPMs that have been installed and their RPM-Version.

Example: AppsTier or DBTier RPM (Redhat Package Manager) Info

```
#-------------------------------------------------------------#
# whatrpm                        Redhat Package Manager (RPM) #
#-------------------------------------------------------------#

openmotif21-2.1.30-11.RHEL4.4.i386
openmotif-devel-2.2.3-9.RHEL4.1.i386
openmotif-2.2.3-9.RHEL4.1.i386
```

About the Authors

Bill Dunham (*Oracle Ace*)

Bill is the founder and principal owner of OATC, Inc. He is a well known Oracle Applications and Technology consultant, having worked with Oracle products since 1985, and Oracle EBS Apps since 1991 (MPL7→R12). His extensive experience with EBS Applications and Technology makes him a trusted advisor to many clients throughout the US and Europe. Bill has worked in many IT and project capacities over the years, mostly focusing as an EBS Program/Project Manager, Architect, Technical/Functional Lead, QA Manager and client advocate. Bill has presented papers at many local and regional Oracle Application Users Group (OAUG) events and at Oracle OpenWorld (OOW). Bill has authored articles for OAUG INSIGHT magazine, as well as co-authored two books, "Special Edition Using Oracle Applications" and "Special Edition Using Oracle 11i." and is co-authoring this new book series called Oracle EBS Applciations *StreetSmarts*®. Bill has designed, developed and authored papers on the "CRP Method" for enterprise application projects. This method focuses on critical and core project activities, all while reducing project costs and focusing on client success. Bill is a member of the Oracle EBS Applications Technology Customer Advisory Board (CAB) for Oracle Corporation, Coordinator for ESOAUG, member of the OAUG GEO/SIG Board, and an Oracle Applications & Applications Technology ACE.

Michael Barone (*Oracle Ace Nominee*)

Michael is an Oracle E-Business Suite Database Administrator with 25 years of IT experience and 16 years of Oracle Applications DBA experience including RAC (Real Application Cluster), ASM (Automatic Storage Management), and Oracle Applications (E-Business Suite). Michael's experience includes full cycle installations and upgrades as well as architecture, installation, administration, upgrade and development of Oracle relational databases. Most recently, Michael has installed, set up, upgraded and administered the production, test, and development databases for major international organizations, federal / state / local government agencies, and manufacturers of hospital equipment, oil-and-gas distribution, automotive-subassemblies, landscape-equipment, diesel-engines, jet-engine turbine blades, medical-equipment, pharmaceuticals, aluminum, concrete, wire and steel products. Michael specializes in upgrading existing Oracle Databases and Oracle Applications and has extensive experience with hot/cold E-Business Suite cloning and backup/restore/disaster-recovery. Michael speaks regularly at Oracle Open World and Oracle Application Users Group (OAUG) Conferences and Oracle Users Group (OUG) Conferences.

ENJOY THE ENTIRE SERIES!

Stay tuned for our next books in the ***StreetSmarts***® series. Our intentions are to release the initial draft of these books and provide subsequent updates as new information is released or we feel that a new releasing a new version is necessary. Please find below, the planned release order (subject to change):

1. **Oracle E-Business Suite StreetSmarts® What Scripts (Version 6.1)**
2. Oracle E-Business Suite StreetSmarts® Unix/Linux Menus (Version 5.0)
3. Oracle E-Business Suite StreetSmarts® Performance Monitoring (Version 2.0)
4. Oracle E-Business Suite StreetSmarts® Functional Analyzers (Version 2.0)
5. Oracle E-Business Suite StreetSmarts® ADOP OnLine Patching ADZD Scripts
6. Oracle E-Business Suite StreetSmarts® CRP Method [Fall 2016]
7. Oracle E-Business Suite StreetSmarts® AutoConfig
8. Oracle E-Business Suite StreetSmarts® Cloning
9. Oracle E-Business Suite StreetSmarts® Upgrades
10. Oracle E-Business Suite StreetSmarts® Purging & Archiving [NEW]

www.ingramcontent.com/pod-product-compliance
Lightning Source LLC
Chambersburg PA
CBHW080931170526
45158CB00008B/2252
9781365822681